TWAYNE'S WORLD AUTHORS SERIES
A Survey of the World's Literature

Sylvia E. Bowman, Indiana University
GENERAL EDITOR

DENMARK

Leif Sjoberg
State University of New York at Stony Brook
EDITOR

Kjeld Abell

TWAS 394

Kjeld Abell

KJELD ABELL

By FREDERICK J. MARKER

University of Toronto

TWAYNE PUBLISHERS

A DIVISION OF G. K. HALL & CO., BOSTON

Library of Congress Cataloging in Publication Data

Marker, Frederick J
  Kjeld Abell.

  (Twayne's world authors series; TWAS 394: Denmark)
  1. Abell, Kjeld, 1901-1961.
PT8175.A25Z76 839.8'1'272 [B]   76-6102 ISBN 0-8057-6236-1

MANUFACTURED IN THE UNITED STATES OF AMERICA

Contents

About the Author

Frederick J. Marker is Professor of English at the University of Toronto, where he has taught English and comparative drama since 1967. His publications include *Hans Christian Andersen and the Romantic Theatre* (1971), *The Scandinavian Theatre: A Short History* (with Lise-Lone Marker, 1975), *The Heibergs* (edited and translated, 1971), a portion of *The Revels History of Drama in English 1750–1880* (with Lise-Lone Marker, 1975), and a recent edition of H. C. Andersen's comedy *Den nye Barselstue* to commemorate the centennial of Andersen's death. He is also the author of several plays and translations as well as a wide variety of scholarly articles in the fields of comparative drama and theatrical history.

Professor Marker was educated at Harvard, the University of Copenhagen (where he held a Fulbright Fellowship), and Yale; he received his doctorate from the Yale School of Drama in 1967. He has a keen interest in the practical theater and has directed numerous productions. He has been the editor of the journal *Modern Drama* since 1972.

Preface

"The theater is always straining in revolt against a theater that has survived theater," the late Donald Oenslager once remarked in a speech. "There is something wrong unless you insist that you do the theater over after your own heart's desire." No critic or student of modern drama, coming upon the plays and theories of Kjeld Abell, can fail to be swept along by the ebullience of an iconoclast who, in the true spirit of Oenslager's felicitous observation, was determined to make the theater of his day over after his own heart's desire. Fifteen years have elapsed since Abell's death in 1961, and only during that time has the full significance of his contribution to twentieth-century Scandinavian drama begun to emerge. He challenged the realistic bias of the post-Ibsen theater in Scandinavia with a veritable fusillade of bold and imaginative theatrical experiments. "It was Kjeld Abell who made the Danish theater living and contemporary," H. C. Branner declared in a memorial tribute to his fellow-writer and friend. "It was Kjeld Abell who created the Danish poetic drama so long sought after. It was Kjeld Abell who exploded the closed box-set" and "dissolved the naturalistic rules of time and place to let us see the dramatic present in its coherence with past and future." In addition to being both a literary pioneer and a remarkable technical innovator, Abell also remained throughout his career a thoughtful and provocative critic of his society.

Although Abell's achievement as a dramatist clearly places him among Scandinavia's most important and most interesting modern writers, no full-length critical study of his work has previously appeared in English. Even in Danish, books about Abell are limited to Frederik Schyberg's short treatment of his earlier plays, first published in 1946, and the collection of commemorative essays which appeared following the dramatist's death. This fact should not, of course, be taken to indicate general disinterest in his own country; on the contrary, a number of stage, radio, and television revivals over the past fifteen years—most recently the immensely successful television production of *Anna Sophie Hedvig* in 1975—have carried Abell's drama to a wider popular audience than ever before. Of his fifteen full-length plays, however, only four (*The Melody that Got Lost, Anna Sophie Hedvig, The Queen on Tour,* and *Days on a Cloud*) are available in English translations—a fact which will inevitably give the reader who has no access to Abell's later, more mature fantasies a distinctly distorted picture of his dramatic development. The aim of the present study is to present a balanced critical discussion and assessment of Abell's dramaturgy, in the hope that this may not only prove useful to students of modern or comparative drama lacking a knowledge of this dramatist's work, but that it may also stimulate fuller and more detailed analyses by specialists already familiar with his writing.

A couple of limitations should be noted. The following chapters will focus chiefly on Abell's work for the theater in its various forms and phases, rather than on his films or travel books (one of which, *Three from Minikoi,* is to be found in a very good English translation). Secondly, the matter of language also imposes certain unavoidable ground rules. While Abell wrote with a poet's keen sense of the rhythms and textures of his language, a detailed analysis of his prose style and linguistic techniques—desirable though it may be—is obviously inappropriate in a book intended primarily for the reader with no knowledge of Danish. Nevertheless, it has always seemed reasonable to assume that it is preferable to read a writer in translation than not to read him at all. Hence, especially in the case of those plays for which no English translation is available, an effort has been made to include a few substantial samples of dialogue in order to illustrate the tone and style of the play under discussion. Except on the rare occasions that are noted, all translations in this volume are by the present author. Though every attempt has been made to capture the flavor as well as the meaning of the original, there are times when Abell's favorite coined phrases and flowing festoons of words simply defy creation of a meaningful English equivalent. To further facilitate understanding, all Danish titles will be referred to throughout in translation, with the original given at the first mention.

Preface

As a playwright, Abell was to an unusual degree attuned to the demands and potentialities of the practical theater. Not a few of the leading roles in his plays mirror the personality and abilities of specific performers—in particular Clara Pontoppidan, Bodil Ipsen, and Bodil Kjer, three of the most gifted Danish actresses of this century. In a comparable sense, the visionary, surrealistic atmosphere of Abell's later dramas is perfectly reflected in the graceful, evocative stage environments created for the plays by such designers as Erik Nordgreen and Helge Refn. Thus, while state history is not a direct concern of this study, it has nevertheless seemed appropriate to draw attention from time to time to the contributions of those artists and performers whose particular abilities lent effective theatrical expression to Abell's work.

In a critical study such as this, the usefulness of contemporary newspaper reviews seems self-evident. The immediacy of a perceptive reviewer's response offers an invaluable guide to the direct impact of a given play on a theater audience. In this regard, one is reminded of John Gassner's repeated observation—certainly accurate in the present instance—that "workaday newspaper reviewers" usually "come off better than the critics who write for recondite publications; the newspapermen report on what they see, whereas esoteric critics see only what they want to discuss." Throughout Kjeld Abell's career, the contemporary press in Denmark was distinguished by a succession of exceptionally able drama reviewers (Schyberg, Borberg, Hans Brix, Harald Engberg, Svend Erichsen, and Svend Kragh-Jacobsen, to mention only the most obvious examples) whose perceptive opening-night notices still must be said to occupy a prominent place in the existing body of Abell criticism.

In the gathering of these and other pertinent sources and texts, I have been aided by the cooperation of a number of institutions; I owe special thanks to the staffs of Universitetsbiblioteket (Copenhagen), Statsbiblioteket (Aarhus), and Roskilde Kommunebibliotek for their help and courtesy. I am extremely grateful to the Canada Council for the Leave Fellowship and subsequent research grant which enabled me to complete this project. Among the individuals from whose help I also benefited, I am especially indebted to *magister* Birgit Gad for her interest and assistance. The many essays and introductions by Elias Bredsdorff on the subject of Abell have been a source of particular inspiration to me. On the editorial side, Professor Leif Sjöberg deserves a warm expression of thanks for his patience and kindness. Above all, my deepest gratitude belongs to my wife Lise-Lone, whose critical insight and enthusiastic encouragement have contributed so much to the making of this book.

FREDERICK J. MARKER

University of Toronto

Chronology

1901   Kjeld Abell born August 25 in the provincial Danish town of Ribe in western Jutland.

1912   August Strindberg dies.

1919   Abell graduates from Metropolitanskolen in Copenhagen; studies art at the Royal Academy of Art until 1922.

1920   Max Reinhardt's epoch-making production of Strindberg's *The Ghost Sonata* is seen at Casino Theater in Copenhagen.

1927   Abell completes his studies at the University of Copenhagen and takes his degree in economics and political science; marries and travels to Paris and London to study and work as a stage designer.

1930   Employed as a stage designer at the Danish Royal Theater, in association with choreographer George Balanchine, during the 1930–1931 season.

1932– Works as a graphic artist with a Copenhagen advertising
1934   agency.

1934   November 20, first ballet, *The Widow in the Mirror*, is produced at the Royal Theater.

1935   September 6, his first play, *The Melody that Got Lost*, opens at Riddersalen Theater.

1936   April 3, his first filmscript, *The Rich Boy*, released by Palladium; December 8, *Eve Serves Her Childhood* opens at the Royal Theater; December 26, an English version of *The Melody that Got Lost* opens in London.

1937   Collaborates on the short revue-comedy, *Mars Takes a Holiday*, which opens at Riddersalen Theater on December 26.

1938   April 25, his version of Dickens's *Oliver Twist* is performed by the Danish School Theater (Skolescenen); he collaborates with Harald Lander on the ballet *Thorvaldsen*, staged at the Royal Theater on November 21.

1939 *Anna Sophie Hedvig* opens at the Royal Theater on New Year's Day; February 3, his cabaret-revue, *Cinderella—and yet,* is performed at Apollo Theater.

1940 February 10, *Judith* is produced by the Royal Theater; April 9, German troops invade and occupy Denmark; May 31, Abell's revue-comedy *Dyveke* opens at Riddersalen Theater; he collaborates with Poul Henningsen on the Apollo Theater revue *The Gods Carry On,* which opened for a short run on September 24.

1941 Elected to the board of directors of Tivoli; April 7, his filmscript *Thanks for Coming, Nick!* is released by Palladium.

1942 Two further Abell films, *The Rain Stopped* and *Put on Glasses—!* are produced by Palladium; he collaborates on three Harald Lander ballets performed at the Royal Theater, *Slaraffenland* (February 21), *Fest-Polonaise* (May 15), and *Spring* (December 15).

1943 March 5, *The Queen on Tour* is staged at the Royal Theater on; August 29, the Nazis declare Denmark in a "state of emergency" and hundreds of hostages from Danish cultural life, including Abell himself, are arrested and interned.

1944 On the evening of January 5, Abell interrupts a Royal Theater performance to remind the audience of the murder of Kaj Munk by the Gestapo the previous night; he is forced to remain underground for the duration of the Occupation.

1945 May 5, Denmark is liberated by Allied forces.

1946 March 1, *Silkeborg* opens at the New Theater.

1947 December 11, *Days on a Cloud* is produced by the Royal Theater.

1948 The Danish Royal Theater celebrates its bicentennial, commemorated on December 18 by Abell's festival play *Lot No. 267 East District;* publication of *Theater Sketches in Easter Weather.*

1949 February 13, *Miss Plinckby's Solitaire* opens at the Royal Theater.

1950 November 12, *Vetsera Does Not Bloom for Everyone* is produced at Frederiksberg Theater; Abell's first journey to the Far East, described in his travel book *Footnotes in the Dust* (published 1951).

1952 First visit to China.

1954   December 16, *The Blue Pekinese* is produced at the Royal Theater.

1955   April 3, *Andersen, or The Fairytale of His Life*, commemorating the 150th anniversary of Hans Christian Andersen's birth, is staged at the Royal Theater.

1956   Abell and his wife again travel to China as passengers on a Swedish freighter.

1957   Publication of the novel *cum* travel book *Three from Minikoi.*

1959   March 17, *The Lady of the Camelias*, Abell's adaptation of the Dumas novel, opens at the New Theater.

1961   March 5, dies suddenly at the age of fifty-nine; November 2, *The Scream*, his last play, is produced posthumously at the Royal Theater.

CHAPTER 1

Kjeld Abell and the Modern Theater

THE European revolt against stage naturalism mounted by such theorists and reformers as Adolphe Appia, Edward Gordon Craig, Vsevolod Meyerhold, Max Reinhardt, and Jacques Copeau was—despite August Strindberg's sweeping renewal of modern drama—relatively late in reaching the Scandinavian countries.[1] Following Strindberg's death in 1912, however, a new generation of directors and designers began to emerge in Scandinavia, responsive to the antinaturalistic demands for simplification, stylization, and suggestion raised by Craig and the adherents of the New Stagecraft. By 1920, the rejection of the constrained "one-sidedness" of naturalism foretold by Pär Lagerkvist in his influential manifesto *Modern Theatre: Points of View and Attack* (1918) was well underway on a broad front. By that date, Per Lindberg and Knut Ström had already begun their epoch-making series of productions at the Lorensberg Theater in Gothenburg; Olof Molander, whose revolutionary Strindberg revivals during the thirties would mark a turning point in the quest for a modern production style in Scandinavia, had just made his directorial debut at Dramaten; and in Copenhagen, the actor-director Johannes Poulsen's festive, Reinhardt-inspired spectacles were beginning to bring the forces of change to bear on the Danish theater. "Dionysus, grant us again a feast! Give us again a temple for intensified life!" proclaimed the Danish critic and playwright Svend Borberg in 1919. "We renounce science and all its deeds, the uniformity of time, place, and action, analysis, logical construction, the false realism and the false psychology, 'parts' and 'points'—and we embrace only the unity of thought, the totality of atmosphere, the artistic composition. Grant us then the intoxication, the ecstacy, the great visions! Grant us again a place of revelations."[2] In Scandinavia as elsewhere, the road to the temple was to take many turns, but the fundamental rediscovery during this

15

period that theater is, above all, theater—neither staged literature nor imitated life—represents the background for Kjeld Abell's own unyielding opposition to the "photographic dictatorship" of naturalism. "The theater must not resemble. The theater must be," Abell continually maintained, and no other Danish playwright of this century has worked more vigorously or effectively than he to explode the circumscribed limits of "the theater's photographic three-act-living-rooms."

Kjeld Abell was born in the provincial town of Ribe, in western Jutland, on August 25, 1901. The son of a schoolteacher, he moved with his family to Odense and subsequently to Copenhagen, where he graduated from Metropolitanskolen in 1919. "At that time, during the last school years," he recalls in an impressionistic little volume of reminiscences entitled *Teaterstrejf i Paaskevejr* (*Theatre Sketches in Easter Weather*), "I knew very little about theater. That is to say, I knew what was playing weeks in advance. Nothing escaped me, not a substitution in the repertory, not a cast change. To the theater itself, though, I never went. Only if I was invited. And when did that ever happen? At the very most a couple of times a year."[3] One such occasion is singled out by him, however, as an experience which, above all else, seems virtually to have formed and focused his theatrical perspective—Max Reinhardt's touring production of *The Ghost Sonata*. The visits of Reinhardt and his smoothly disciplined company had already given Scandinavia its first glimpses of the new ideas and techniques that were reshaping twentieth-century European theater.[4] Especially influential were his controversial Strindberg revivals, which opened the eyes of young innovators like Lindberg and Lagerkvist to the visionary, musical power of Strindberg's later dream plays. Reinhardt's boldly expressionistic *Gespenstersonate*, seen in Stockholm in 1917, was repeated at Copenhagen's Casino Theater in 1920, again starring Paul Wegener as a ghastly and terrifying Hummel ("His ice-cold voice cut through the fever-hot atmosphere that streamed forth from the house," Abell remarks in his vivid description of the performance.) It should come as little surprise that this particular Reinhardt production, which blended the frightening, grotesque, and confusing elements of Strindberg's play into what critics called "a nightmare of marionettes," would make so indelible an impression upon the receptive young theatergoer. "I ceased to think. During the brief moments in which the catastrophe took place, there was only time to feel. I felt with my eyes, my ears, my whole being," he tells us. "For me, *The Ghost Sonata* was not an answer but a breath that filled the theater's space and caused it to live, live in a question, caused me to live in that question."[5]

Abell's momentous encounter with Reinhardt's intense, hypnotic approach to Strindberg fostered in him a lasting affinity for the Swedish playwright's work—he even proceeded at once, he recalls, to read ("as though obsessed") volume after volume of Strindberg's collected writings. The experience also seems to have crystallized his repudiation of what Lagerkvist had called "the typical Ibsen drama with its silent tramping on carpets throughout five long acts of words, words, words."[6] Abell's antagonism did not in any sense extend to Ibsen himself, however: "Ibsen was a rebel. Still is one today. . . . He forced [his audience] to look at something they did not want to see, something no one was ever supposed to have seen. But to make matters worse, others were watching at the same time. Had paid to watch. Suddenly the cozy theater of red plush was transformed into a threat against the establishment."[7] Nevertheless, the vital challenge which the naturalistic revolt had once represented had, in Abell's view, been vitiated by the stagnating effects of habit and convention; the drawing-room drama of the post-Ibsen era had congealed "into a picture which with its wealth of correct details left nothing to the audience—the audience was not allowed to be an active part of the endeavor."[8]

A full fifteen years would pass, meanwhile, before the eager young visitor to the Reinhardt guest performance was ready to put his own embryonic conception of a revolutionized theater into practice. Although biography will not be a significant concern in this study, the 1920s were obviously restless and searching years for Abell, crucial for the direction which the development of his talent would take. After his graduation from Metropolitanskolen, he studied art for a time at the Royal Academy of Art before embarking on the demanding degree course in economics and political science offered at the University of Copenhagen. The pressure of his hyper-conservative provincial upbringing made him a conscientious student, though his predilections clearly led him elsewhere. He began during his student years to try his hand at playwriting, and he was also permitted to follow the design work and attend an occasional rehearsal at the Royal Theater. However, in 1927, following conferral of the degree of *cand (idatus) polit(ices)*, Abell immediately departed for Paris and London to study and work as a freelance artist and stage designer—a flight, he later called it, from the oppressive realities of "conditions at home" and an academic training in which he had not the remotest interest. His prolonged *Wanderjahr* during the period 1927–1930 may be regarded as his theatrical apprenticeship. Its most negative aspect is embodied in his disenchanted and angry reaction to the mechanized commercialism of the newly built Théâtre Pigalle ("outside a monstrosity of cement and nakedness, inside a more or less cunning hotchpotch of various long-established practices"); here he made his stage debut in a creaky historical pageant by Sacha Guitry, and briefly found work as a supernumerary. Hardly more enlightening was his frustrated encounter, a few years later, with the stolid music-hall conservatism of Sir Oswald Stoll's Alhambra Theater in London, where he functioned for a time as a scene painter. In a more positive sense, however, these years abroad exposed him to a wide spectrum of more fruitful influences and impressions—including René Clair's brilliant film satires of the *petit-bourgeosie*, Diaghilev's Ballets Russes, and the "picturesque" theater of Louis Jouvet ("theater as a framework for the spoken word, a background for the spoken word, a springboard for the spoken word"[9])—all of which would come to play a part in the making of a dramatist.

Kjeld Abell's emergence as a playwright coincides roughly with the broad revival of Danish drama that took place during the period between the two World Wars. During the course of the twenties and thirties, native playwriting was gradually enriched by a generation of new writers whose sources of antinaturalistic inspiration included German expressionism, symbolism, Pirandello, and Freud.[10] After 1920, Borberg's exhilarating vision of the theater as "a place of revelations" and a "temple for intensified life" began to infuse a wide variety of new Danish plays, including Borberg's own expressionistic experiments, the clever intellectual satires of Sven Clausen, and, above all, the sweeping "heroic" dramas of Kaj Munk, with their focus on a lusty world beyond good and evil, where (in Munk's own words) "heads toppled, brains burst, and limbs were shattered." By the mid-thirties, the imaginative psychological and social dramas of Carl Erik Soya and Leck Fischer had begun to add further substance to this promising dramatic renaissance. In retrospect, relatively little of the work of these playwrights seems perhaps to have retained any lasting literary interest. Munk, Abell's eminent contemporary, clearly represents the one notable exception. However, while the courageous poet-priest remained, until his death at the hands of the Nazis in 1944, Abell's closest rival for popularity and critical acclaim, his ambitious and passionate historical works, heavy with echoes of Oehlenschläger and Shakespeare, could not have presented more of an antithesis to Abell's playful verbal elegance and innovative structural experiments.

In general, astonishing technical virtuosity coupled with a prolific ability to devise new and provocative forms of theater are the qualities which set Abell's contribution apart from that of any other playwright of his generation in Scandinavia. "Why is there anything in the theater called realism?" he demanded in a seminal essay from the thirties. "Can theater ever be realistic? Has 'the human comedy' anything to do with everyday reality? Where should the sofa stand? Has the placement of the desk never anything to do with the position of the window? Must the actors always stand facing the audience? . . . Who has decreed how reality should look? Does it always look like that?"[11] As his art deepened, the questions multiplied, and their urgency seemed to increase. Underlying his restless quest for an imaginative and "retheatricalized" theater is the fundamental purpose to which he incessantly returns in his theoretical writing: to restore the spectator, narcotized by the literal-mindedness of the naturalistic style, to his rightful function as an active participant in the theatrical event. The audience is, for Abell, the "fully worthy opponent against whom the struggle must be taken up—with all the unreal theatrical devices and theatrical effects; victory must be won on both sides of the footlights—or rather, the barrier of the footlights should instead be felt to be eliminated—and in the midst of this battlefield of cardboard, painted cloth, and makeup, the true reality shall stand vigorously alive."[12]

CHAPTER 2

Social Comedy and Satire

I *Abell and Ballet*

IN his search for a suitable mode of theatrical expression, Kjeld
Abell turned first to the ballet. The choice is not a very surprising one—during his formative years in the Paris of the late 1920s the
young university graduate, certain only that he had no intention of
making use of his degree, was exposed to Sergei Diaghilev's Russian
ballet troupe at the height of its powers. He became acquainted
with Diaghilev's brilliant balletmaster George Balanchine, designed
costumes for the first tour of the talented young ballerina Nini
Theilade, and found himself fascinated in general by the world of
the dance. With Diaghilev's death in 1929, his Ballets Russes disbanded and Balanchine accepted an invitation to spend a guest
season at the Danish Royal Theater. Abell joined the choreographer
in Copenhagen, and was associated with him as a set and costume
designer at the Royal Theater during the great Balanchine season of
1930–1931. "Abell's designs caught the imagination with their simple refinement, their bold tastefulness, and their airy charm," critic
Frederik Schyberg was later moved to declare. "A new theater
designer of international stature" had emerged.[1]

Even if one is perhaps no longer quite so impressed by the "simple refinement" or "airy charm" of Abell's early set designs, his
initial engagement as the designer of five of Balanchine's ballets
nevertheless had a profound influence on the direction of his development. For the first of the two full-evening programs devoted to
the guest choreographer's work (opening October 12, 1930), Abell
provided both costumes and settings for two of Leonide Massine's
best-known ballet compositions, "The Three-Cornered Hat" and
"La Boutique fantasque." Reminiscences of the latter work—in
which Massine had in 1919 adopted a fresh approach to the tradi-

tional animated toy shop motif by giving his toys character and thus avoiding the pitfalls of purely mechanical movement—are especially evident in the playwright's own later fantasies, most notably in *Eve Serves Her Childhood*. For the season's second Balanchine evening (opening January 18, 1931), Abell supplied designs for all three of the works presented: Balanchine's athletic Stravinsky ballet "Apollon Musagetes," a miscarried production of the Sicilian burlesque "Barabau," and the Balanchine rendering of the older Mikhail Fokine-Richard Strauss ballet "Joseph's Legend," in which Abell substituted an imaginative Egyptian fantasy decor for the Italian Renaissance style of the original Fokine version.[2]

Although peripheral, in a strictly literary sense, to Abell's achievement as a dramatist, these early encounters with the modern ballet theater deserve notice chiefly because of their significant effect on his attitude toward the nature of the theatrical event. A balletic emphasis on nonverbal means of expression—music, dance, plastic art, pantomime, gesticulation—is in many ways as intrinsic to Abell's theater as it is, for example, to Artaud's—though in Abell's case it led neither to the extreme "hieratic style" nor the radical subordination of dialogue demanded by the French theorist. Three years after the Balanchine season, Abell's preoccupation with ballet as a medium for the expression of ideas reached its highpoint with "Enken i Spejlet" ("The Widow in the Mirror"), an expressionistic and highly experimental modern ballet which marked his debut as a dramatic author.

In a technical sense, the new ballet was an audacious, Balanchine-inspired attempt at renewal by its author and its talented young choreographer, Børge Ralov, and represented a deliberate break with the conventional Bournonville style of the Danish ballet. Ballet, Abell proclaimed in an interview shortly after the opening on November 20, 1934, must "be dance! Or movement—everything must be able to be expressed through dance in harmony with music. There are many who claim that 'Widow' is not ballet—but at all events it contains movement from beginning to end, and my idea or opinion is that in ballet composition we must avoid pantomime. Ballet must in no sense be pantomime."[3] Far more revolutionary than its technique, however, was the topical, satirical tone of this contemporary ballet's social content—a tone that gives it a distinct affinity with Brecht's bitter choreographic parable "The Seven Deadly Sins." The Brecht-Weill ballet, which Balanchine had staged in London as "Anna-Anna" the previous year and Abell had evidently once hoped to design for its Copenhagen production, met with a storm of "anti-communist" opposition in Denmark and was finally seen at the Royal Theater for two furiously denounced performances in 1936. Schyberg's review in *Berlingske Tidende* (November 13, 1936) of this important production draws an enlightening generic comparison between it and the Abell ballet which, at least in a chronological sense, prepared the way for it: "the action, the fable itself is the chief element, and the art of ballet is a subordinate, almost an eliminated feature." One step further and ballet has abolished itself, the critic adds, but "both in 'Seven Deadly Sins' and in 'Widow' the balance is maintained. *Theater* has still resulted from the experiments. A rather strange, rough, but living theater."[4]

Although it would be misleading to range Abell's youthful experiment alongside Brecht's trenchant and mature work, "The Widow in the Mirror" is nevertheless of considerable interest as a succinct pantomimic prelude to one of the most persistent themes in Abell's writing: the conflict between the forces of life and the oppressive, destructive constraints of social conventionality. In his ballet, this theme is stated in a series of concise and striking visual images. A young woman is married with all the customary trivial ceremonies; at the wedding, her "better self"—an alter ego called simply the Adagio Bride—dances with her dream lover, but both disappear and leave the newlyweds to sail into the dull gray conventionality of their daily existence aboard the "Everyday Ship." Their empty life together is a monotonous "Pax de six banale"—an endless social dance of trivial figures, interrupted by the occasional glimpse of brutality and unpleasantness. Outside the wife's garden, life may appear, in the guise of a ragged beggar, but she has nothing left to offer him except the remains of her wedding cake. One day her indifferent husband dies, and her role in society is apparently finished—her completed life's portrait, which is in the process of being painted by an artist throughout the ballet, is presented to her as an empty frame wreathed in black mourning crape! Her obliviousness to the living world of colorful machines and dancing workers surrounding her—effectively expressed by Ralov in an ironic gavotte in which she walks, uncomprehendingly, over and around this swirling mass of humanity without ever succeeding in penetrating it—makes her bury herself in her past and her self-preoccupation (the mirror), and she is left to dance a shadow dance with the stage props of memory. In the closing moments of the work, however, the Adagio Bride returns to reunite the widow with the symbolic beggar—the rather obvious image of life's strength and vigor—whom she had previously rejected.

The ballet's principal problem lies in the abrupt and gratuitous "resolution" of its main conflict. Abell's involved visual symbolism, often startlingly apt but occasionally either capricious or obscure, could well be expected to outrage the more conservative elements of the traditional ballet public; the "average audience," warned *BT* (November 21, 1934), "surely goes to the ballet to see speed and color and youth and beauty—and they got all these things last evening—but they have no wish to be distracted in their enjoyment by being confronted with problems which not even the author has managed to solve." A more analytical critic such as Schyberg was able, however, to cut through to the dramaturgical heart of the matter—namely, an unhappy tendency in Abell's work to allow an unmotivated and hastily tacked-on resolution to dissipate utterly the powerful sense of dramatic tension he has so carefully sought to build up. "His point is present on paper," Schyberg argued in his review of "The Widow in the Mirror,"

but dramatically it does not exist. A point is not made by letting a character or two exit right. The stage demands development. The old-fashioned ballets had their finale, which consisted of a whirl, a highpoint, a culmination of dancing. If one wishes to abandon this traditional conclusion, it can only be done by creating instead an intellectual highpoint, an emotional release in the audience's mind which stands in place of the finale. *The whirl must be turned loose within the spectator.* If it is absent, the curtain will fall without motivation, creating a pause of dissatisfaction before the applause can begin.[5]

These valid critical reservations notwithstanding, however, no one could overlook the abundant ability which radiated from Abell's talented experiment. It is, of course, patently absurd to separate the libretto of a ballet from its musical and choreographic realization in production, and the success of the new work, retained in the Danish ballet's repertoire for twenty-two performances, derived in large measure from Børge Ralov's inventive choreography, Bernhard Christensen's congenial musical score, and, above all, the dazzling execution of such internationally important dancers as Ulla Poulsen,

Ralov himself, and Margot and Harald Lander. Nevertheless, the impact of Abell's remarkable dramatic situation in a sense over-shadows the production itself, heralding as it does both a new direction in modern ballet composition and the emergence of a new dramatist. "A theater poet was born," Schyberg later remarked, "but was he mute?"[6]

Abell's powers of speech were amply demonstrated the following year by the phenomenal success of his first play, *The Melody that Got Lost*. Though first and foremost an exponent of rich dramatic language, however, the versatile playwright continued for a number of years to work actively in nonverbal ballet theater as well. On four occasions he collaborated with Harald Lander, this period's most renowned Danish choreographer and balletmaster—most notably in "Thorvaldsen" (1938), Lander's adept festival ballet commemorating the hundredth anniversary of the great sculptor's triumphant return to Copenhagen. Abell not only designed the setting but also devised the ballet's simple but effective framework. The action is little more than a playful reprise of the plot device in *Eve Serves Her Child-hood:* the famous statues in Thorvaldsen's Museum—Venus, Mars, Hercules, Apollo, Hebe, the Graces, Ganymede, and Vulcan—suddenly spring to life before the eyes of a blasé, ultramodern American tourist (Margot Lander) who has been caught in the museum after closing time. When a choreographic duel ensues between the attractions of classical ballet and modern jazz dance techniques, the outcome, in an Abell fable, is not difficult to predict. The hero, Thorvaldsen's mighty Jason (Børge Ralov), succumbs completely to the charms of the modern intruder, finally exchanging his golden fleece for a fashionable suit and trench coat before deserting the museum with her. "What about Thorvaldsen? The authors have evidently forgotten about him, but since it is a commemorative performance they send his statue up through the trapdoor, and Margot presents him with a mixed bouquet (renewed applause)," wrote the disgruntled Viggo Cavling in *Politiken* (November 22, 1938). However, neither Cavling's displeasure nor Hans Brix's good-natured irony ("an extremely nice, atmospheric, and cleverly contrived dance tribute to the master of the plastic arts, full of solemnity and white statues . . ."[7]) had a material effect on the popular acceptance of this lively and serviceable balletic homage.

By 1942, the year in which Abell again worked with Lander on three new ballets at the Royal Theater, the dramatist had already completed four major plays and had moved from the social comedies and satires of the thirties to a cluster of plays dealing with the serious and highly relevant theme of individual human responsibility in the face of tyranny. Accordingly, his involvement in his three final ballets for the Royal Theater company[8]—he wrote the scenario for "Slaraffenland" (February 21), designed "Fest-Polonnaise" (May 15), and both wrote and designed "Vaaren" ("Spring") (December 15)—seems to a greater extent tangential to the main line of his work. However, these ballets, like his film scripts from this period, offer noteworthy glimpses of characteristic concerns and techniques at a time when the Nazi occupation had effectively curtailed free expression in his principal medium. In "Fest-Polonnaise," for example, his stage design for "an immense white ballroom in a fantasy Amalienborg," at the rear of which one glimpsed an evocative stylized rendering of Saly's renowned equestrian statue of Frederik V, was "a masterpiece of decorative art"[9] that added its own moving comment to Lander's politically charged and brilliantly executed tribute to the thirtieth anniversary of the beloved King Christian X's reign. The Abell-Lander ballet "Spring," danced to Grieg's music and ostensibly depicting the bitter rigors of a Norwegian winter, was in reality an even more thinly disguised political allegory of Nazi oppression and terror in Norway. Abell's starkly simple design concept—a single set piece with a huge gate with heavy iron chains, crushed beneath snow and ice—was a visual image of the ballet's implied political comment on the chilling inhumanity and crushing brutality of the aggressor. This particular example illustrates clearly the strong feeling for plastic imagery that drew Abell—as it had drawn the painter-playwright Jean Cocteau—to the ballet.

The interplay between ballet and theater is thus a significant factor in Abell's early career. Not only did he seek to apply his ideas for theatrical reform to the ballet, attempting to revitalize the heritage of the Danish ballet by snatching "Bournonville's spectacles"— "fogged by the past and by an unholy need to be carried away by sentiments that are rooted for the most part in tradition and all which that implies"—off the noses of the general ballet public.[10] In its turn, his exposure to "the wordless theater" of ballet taught him to control "theatrical space, the abstract, invisible space, spatial balance created by the precision of movement and the will of the silent word."[11] Ballet-drama sharpened and extended the range of his ability to integrate nonverbal elements and effective visual imagery into his theatrical poetry. From the very outset, in *The Melody that Got Lost*, a lively interaction between the verbal and nonverbal elements of drama was one of his most distinctive traits as a playwright.

II   The Melody that Got Lost *(1935)*

"Talent, Talent, Talent," proclaimed the double-column headline of one typical review of Kjeld Abell's *Melodien, der blev væk (The Melody that Got Lost)*, which opened at the small experimental Riddersalen Theater on September 6, 1935. The date remains a memorable one in the history of Danish theater. As the inaugural production in the avant-garde director Per Knutzon's influential management of Riddersalen, the play's unprecedented run of 594 performances between 1935 and 1937 marked an emphatic breakthrough for the antinaturalistic, "retheatricalized," and socially relevant style of theater which both Abell and Knutzon championed. From an international perspective, *Melody* remains among Abell's best known and most widely performed plays—though its English translation, produced in London at the suburban Embassy Theatre during the 1936–1937 season, is in fact a disappointingly unpoetic and often directly inaccurate rendering of the crisp and earthy colloquialism of the original.[12]

The loosely structured, revuelike style of Abell's first play was perfectly suited to Riddersalen's restricted physical dimensions and its popular cabaret traditions. Brecht, whose play *Die Rundköpfe und die Spitzköpfe (The Roundheads and the Peakheads)* received its controversial world premiere at Knutzon's Riddersalen in 1936, has described its physical properties with characteristic precision: "Smoking and eating are allowed in the theater. It provides 220 seats. The stage is 21 feet wide, 24 feet deep, and 30 feet in height."[13] However, Brecht's uncompromisingly stark and politically explosive "atrocity story" proved much less palatable to Riddersalen audiences than Abell's lighter and more conciliatory social satire. The young Danish playwright exploited to the fullest the close, informal rapport between Riddersalen's modest platform stage and its smoking and drinking cabaret audience, and he developed a vocabulary of evocative visual effects which were compatible with the theater's simple means—a wedding is represented by a bridal veil, a bouquet, and a top hat moving across the stage on a wire amid offstage cheers and shouting; a depressingly trite honeymoon becomes simply a waiter beside a table taking the same unimaginative order over and over ("two asparagus soup, two chicken, Melba icecream") while a voice booms out the passing train stations. The play, wrote Svend Borberg in *Politiken* (September 7, 1935), "teems throughout with effects which in their easily understood symbolism can only be characterized as 'brilliant'—they are so fresh and so new."

In its style, Abell's comedy partakes freely of the techniques—though not the tortured and pessimistic *Weltanschauung*—of expressionism. In an article published in 1935, Abell argued that Danish theater had "sprung over an entire epoch in theatrical history, the expressionistic. One can say what one will about it, good or bad, but it brought about the necessary renewal which led the theater back to true theater."[14] In *Melody*, the dramatist-designer skilfully manipulates the familiar devices of expressionism—depersonalized, allegorical characters, skeletal and distorted settings, truncated and violently antirealistic scenes, startling juxtapositions. Above all, however, he puts the expressionist's vision of subjectively distorted, mechanistic reality to effective comic and satirical use. The entire play, as a Brechtian street-singer tells us in an opening ballad, takes the shape of "a song about a man named Larsen, / him you meet on the street every day,"[15] and it is through the eyes of this expressionistically archetypal everyman that the bewildering vicissitudes of life are viewed. Larsen, a virtual embodiment of the thirties in whom one can also perceive kinship with Erich Kästner's characters, with the rebellious clerks of Georg Kaiser and Elmer Rice, and the "little man" of countless chaplinades, is brought face to face with the fundamental Abellian dilemma—the choice between a free and open espousal of life and an abject submission to the deadly formulae of middle-class conventionality and respectability. The visual and musical expression of this conflict in "The Widow in the Mirror" is here given the added dimension of richly vernacular dramatic language.

Abell's social allegory is conveyed with the swift strokes and primary colors of a modernized fairy tale. In his dreary job ("something between a superior office boy and an inferior head clerk") Larsen shares an office with three identically masked automaton-typists (all called Miss Miller), who spend their coffee breaks fatuously admiring "Lord Wynnforth," a purely illusory film-magazine

idealization of elegance and romance who is rolled in and out on
wheels at appropriate moments. Unlike the spiritually lobotomized
Miss Millers and their tyrannical boss, however, Larsen is able to
respond spontaneously to the insistent melody which he can hear
"wandering through the city singing and whistling"—the melody of
life beyond the office, "where you don't have to wear a collar and
tie, and you can say whatever you please, and the time is whatever
you want it to be"(14).

Determined to be a "tear-off daily calendar" no longer, Abell's
rebellious clerk deserts his post and sets off hand in hand with his
fiancée Edith to pursue the melody, and to "make an uproar in the
portières" and "tear down all the old family pictures" in her parents'
stuffy bourgeois home. In a scene aptly titled "Picture of Mother
and Dad," Larsen's future in-laws are, quite literally, depicted as a
grotesque, cartoonlike family portrait:

*The curtain parts, and the setting is a huge cabinet photograph, showing
Edith's parents sitting at a table beside which is a dreadful floor lamp. She is
massive and important; he is quite small and his feet do not reach the floor.
Holes are cut in the backcloth for the actors' faces, their bodies being
painted on the cloth.* (23)

Their means of convincing Larsen to reconsider his impulsive rebellion are primitive but effective:

MOTHER.   . . . You can do what you like. Of course in a way I'm glad to
    be keeping you at home, little Edith.
EDITH.   You talk as though I'll never ever get married.
MOTHER.   Well, it's certainly a long way off. Now that your young man
    intends to float along through the air listening to whatever melodies he
    might happen to hear, he won't have much left for a down payment on an
    apartment. By the way, I saw a nice little apartment the other day, just
    right for the two of you—charming and not beyond reach—and I was just
    saying to your father that we really wouldn't mind helping you with fifty
    crowns a month. That would actually be quite a substantial help—and
    there's plenty in your savings account for a bedroom suite—and we might
    even lend a hand with the instalments on a living room. I had intended
    you to have the piano—
LARSEN.   But you don't seem to understand—
MOTHER.   Oh yes, I do. But it's still true that what's bright scarlet in the
    evening ends up being pale pink in the morning. Isn't that so, Carl?
                                                                        (24–25)

This formidable matriarch's relentless recital of hope-chest materialism—sheets, monogrammed table linen, rosebud china, "chateau-pattern" coffee spoons, and all the rest of it—drones on. "Lucky they're all things that won't spoil by keeping," she concludes:

But that white satin your American cousin sent you had better be exchanged for something darker. You'll be a bit old to be a real bride. (*Silence. Father coughs. Silence.*) (25)

Larsen is crushed ("an inventory list like that would take the gas out of anybody's balloon"), and at last promises, for the sake of Edith and the social conformity required to possess her, never again to sing, listen for, or even remember the melody. This fateful abjuration, punctuated by a loud thunderclap, reinforces the play's fairy-tale tone; Larsen must now endure the consequences of his ill-considered choice. Edith's ineffectual Father, precursor of the emasculated and sterile Daddy figures of absurd drama, draws a disturbing moral from the would-be icon smasher's abrupt capitulation:

You were coming home to tear down all the old family pictures. Yes, it's easy enough to take them off the nail, but unfortunately there's always a faded spot underneath—and that offends our instinctive sense of propriety—it looks messy—and so we hang them back up again. Oh, well. (29)

Thus, the point—sometimes misstated in cursory summaries of the play and perhaps somewhat obscured by its English title—is *not* that Larsen involuntarily "loses" his life-sustaining melody, but that he wilfully shuts it out and dispossesses himself of it; and the crime of self-dispossession is regarded as seriously in Abell's world as it is in O'Neill's. In this light, then, the comedy takes on a quasi-classical format as Larsen—called "a kind of industrialized parallel to the older rural culture's Jeppe on the Hill" by one critic[16]—is brought to taste the bitter fruits of his folly.

By means of a kaleidoscope of scenes that often resemble short revue sketches, Abell sets the treadmill of his protagonist's dispirited middle-class existence in motion. The stylized "Danse du Bureau" of a monotonous nine-to-five office routine is "relieved" only by the paralyzing tedium of Sundays "at rest in the lap of the family with your head in a cup of coffee and your feet on a roll of pastry" (38). Larsen is taught the futility of his petty ambitiousness in a grotesquely imagined sequence entitled "Chanson du Bureau"—a concise and characteristic example of this playwright's blend of expressionism and absurdity:

LARSEN *sings (operatic aria):*

The day has come,	For Hansen's been fired,
Now it must be,	His desk stands there empty,
Luck will turn,	I shall advance,
Trouble will cease,	Money will flow,
Today is the day,	His job shall be mine,
The day of all days,	His job shall be mine,
Yes, today.	Yes, his job.

Entrance march. The boss's wife is shown in—a window-display dummy hung with jewels, handbag, silver fox, etc. Duet between the boss and a clarinet:

BOSS.   Good morning, my dear,
           And what brings you here,
           To visit my humble office?
CLARINET *plays fairly peacefully.*
BOSS.   The job left by Hansen.
           Well, I've several in mind.
CLARINET *plays excitedly.*
BOSS.   Cousin Heinrich, hm—do you think that it's really his line?
CLARINET *plays ingratiatingly.*
BOSS.   Well—I'm afraid that I'm not really sure.
CLARINET *works itself up and becomes hysterical.*
BOSS.   Of course, my dear, I know you're right.
           Heinrich's the man for the job!
CLARINET *becomes calm again.*
The boss embraces the dummy. Blackout—one spot on Larsen's disillusioned face behind the window.

(36–37)

The horror of Larsen's sham existence without the melody reaches a climax in the scene entitled "Sunday"—a witty fantasia of trivial domestic rituals described by one reviewer as "a coup of comic invention with its simultaneously corrosive yet touching satire of Sunday pleasures and family gatherings."[17] As a unit, the three connected family scenes at the center of the play mark its turning point. During their hilariously bucolic Sunday stroll in the woods ("Nature's really about the best thing we've got, and the greatest"), Edith tries without success to explain her frustration to her domineering mother, while Larsen, who is left behind with a sympathetic elf, reflects on the fact that "they've amputated me someplace or other, and it isn't anything that will grow back again" (48). After these futile attempts at communication, however, the family relapses into listless, nerve-racking silence—*"Father begins to drum the Radetsky March with his fingers on the table, whistles it under his breath, continuing for a long, long time"* (51)—until an irate spectator (predictably named Larsen) emerges from the audience to confront the cast, a stagehand, and even Per Knutzon himself with his demand for some positive action:

Do you think I've come here to watch nice, decent people becoming more and more miserable? . . . When I go to the theater I want to see something that ends just a little happily. . . . This sort of thing has no end. If it's the author's intention to keep things true to life, then this gloom can go on forever without the slightest variation. . . . No, no, my dear sir, if you won't do anything about it, I will. Things can damn well not go on like this any longer! (52–53)

This deliberately contrived, Pirandellian intrusion from the "real" world represents not only, as Schyberg phrases it, a good example of Abell's "consistent effort to activate his audience and provoke them into finding their own solutions."[18] It also marks a conscious shift of focus and distance, moving the play from the "illusion" of dramatic development (or lack of it) to the "reality" of epic argument and change. This movement is reflected as well in Edith's subsequent vehement decision to overthrow the prearranged script and "say just whatever I please"—to which Knutzon replies, "Very well, we'll play it however you wish." On this "improvisational" note, Edith seizes the active role and determines, on behalf of the countless Mrs. Larsens who appear in the windows of the houses around her, to rescue Larsen from his passive indifference and sexual lifelessness by recovering the lost melody—"if I have to tear it up out of the city streets with my bare hands" (57).

Following this strong comic peripety, however, the play falters and loses its way; despite their enthusiasm, most of the reviewers expressed various reservations about its relatively weak second act—and one is not inclined to disagree with them. The family's hectic and disorganized search for the elusive melody, which is always right there before them in the shape of three invisible "Melody Maidens," is dramatized in a rambling sequence of short episodes (the parents' farcical visit to a Lost and Found Office, Larsen's appeals to caricatured representations of Death and Nature, and so on) which often, in the words of one critic, "both efface the idea of the play and also render it rather long-winded."[19] Even Schyberg, Abell's staunchest champion, is forced to concede that "the action which at the beginning was so concrete now becomes abstract and incoherent, very charming but completely disjointed."[20] The comic action regains its direction and equilibrium only after the focus has returned to Edith, who encounters a little girl (her former unspoiled self?) skipping rope and singing the vagrant melody of life. The remainder of the play depicts Edith's symbolic unravelling—as she gropes her way hand over hand along a huge red skipping rope—of the melody's mystery.

Abell is at pains to ensure that the didactic heart of the mystery is laid bare. The class-conscious workman whom Edith encounters and who at first rudely bars her path is a willing and loquacious spokesman for the playwright's collectivist moral. His robust and untranslatably colloquial tirades against the unconcerned, selfish, inhibited, tradition-bound bourgeoisie foretell one of Abell's most persistent thematic preoccupations: "You've got your noses blocked up and your eyes bound shut and your skin and hide have grown together with your underpants. Whoever the hell made you in his own image must have had something to do with the dry goods business" (84). When the audience member again intervenes—and recognizes none other than Per Knutzon in the role of the workman—he is told in round and colorful terms to "buzz off home":

Home on the bookshelf and take a stroll with the past. That's good enough for the likes of you. . . . Now you get a move on, and fast. I've heard tell, and I think it's probably right too, that you're one of these here spectators—and if there's one thing I hates it's them folks what sits around just lookin' on. (82)

When Edith discovers the melody in the clank of the laborer's tools, he allows her to take it with her—on the condition that she and Larsen will return to "sing it together with us."

Although Edith encounters and appropriates more of the melody's outward "signs"—the harmonica of a carefree bohemian on a bicycle, the glasses of a football-playing professor of natural science—its collectivist refrain is already abundantly clear. A purely individual rebellion against social forms is, by itself, not sufficient. "To be truly able to sing the melody," explained Sven Møller Kristensen, author of the play's song lyrics, "one must work together with others, 'not I for you, nor you for me, but *we* for *us*,' as it says in the closing song." Larsen, who has in the meantime decisively settled accounts with the respectable coward he once was ("so afraid of everything, of losing his job, of getting rain on his good suit, of anything at all") and has discarded his respectable clothes at the police station where he has been held for creating a disturbance, is now ready to receive the blessing of Edith's discovery. His "rebirth" is graphic, as Edith hauls him in at the end of her long red skipping rope / umbilical cord for a final vigorous chorus of the song of life. The play's optimistic resolution is, however, ultimately more accidental than organic, and hence less than satisfying. "Its logic did not ring true," Schyberg writes, "because the perspective of the action is pushed forward into the future, as a postulate," and Larsen's problem is never really resolved in dramatic terms.[21]

As a characteristic expression of, and response to, the universal dislocation that convulsed the society of the 1930s, Abell's fervent *evangelium* parallels Clifford Odets' passionate plea, carved from *Isaiah*, to "awake and sing, ye that dwell in dust." Though the young dramatist might insist, four days after the opening of *The Melody that Got Lost*, that he "takes absolutely no programmatic political position whatsoever,"[22] his play's "revolutionary" social message is hammered home with a didactic clarity that would make Brecht blush. Nevertheless, its more conservative reviewers strove manfully to save it from the leftwing "stigma." "The courage and the joy of life with which the play resounds are so attractive that, even though we hate everything that smacks of communism, we must still forgive the author his little collectivist excess at the end," pronounced *BT*. "For isn't it wonderful to meet a man who looks at life and finds it beautiful and good?" In his zeal to avoid "ending before Lenin's altar," Svend Borberg was moved to declare in *Politiken* that the "true" theme of Abell's "juggling act with abstractions" was "that man lives not by bread alone, and that only the little, idiotic *superfluity*—the frill, if you like—makes life's tedious necessities bearable. One has the feeling of, having witnessed a wild battle on the barricades after which, when the smoke has cleared, all things stand magically untouched and at their most comfortable." If these critics seem wilfully to miss the serious intent behind Abell's amiable comic allegory, however, they also obfuscate the nature of his "political" involvement. Like Odets, Abell possessed an ambiguous, lyrical talent that would prove trying to any coherent political ideology. His socially critical works conform perhaps best to Joseph Wood Krutch's definition of a "revolutionary" play, as one which "invents its morality" and involves a reevaluation of the audience's attitude toward moral, intellectual, or social questions.[23] A poetic and emotional adherence to the spirit of revolt runs through all of Abell's work, and it is this quality, rather than any objectified, programmatic philosophy, which lends expressiveness and significance to his writing. The melody that gets lost in his first play is heard again, in a variety of modes and keys, in all his later ones.

III   Eve Serves Her Childhood (1936)

With his imaginative and highly unorthodox burlesque *Eva aftjener sin barnepligt* (*Eve Serves Her Childhood*), Abell "graduated" as a playwright from the tiny cabaret dimensions of Riddersalen to the far greater challenge of the Royal Theater on Kongens Nytorv. In this large space, quipped Schyberg in his *Berlingske Tidende* review of the new work, his *Melody* would "have simply gotten lost in the gulf between the stage and the auditorium, would have disappeared in the orchestra pit—where in a way, of course, it also belongs."[24] Critical misgivings about the young playwright's ability to cope with the demands of the larger theater were, however, quickly laid to rest. *Eve*, which opened on December 8, 1936 in Holger Gabrielsen's gracefully ironic mise-en-scène, scored one of the first complete victories on the Danish national stage for the radically antinaturalistic techniques which were reshaping the Scandinavian theater at this time.[25]

In this freewheeling theatrical cartoon, Abell seems determined to exploit every facility and every trapdoor at the theater's disposal. "His world," remarked one observer, "is the theater's world of childish improbabilities and unrealities, of all its symbols—peopled with human beings, yet viewed with that foreshortening which is the theater's."[26] Thematically, the new play leveled much of its attack at familiar targets already strafed in its author's two earlier works: the prejudices of stereotypical middle-class respectability, family tyranny, the deadly effects of dead ideas and outmoded values. In terms of tone and form, however, *Eve* represents a major development in the shaping of what Schyberg aptly calls the dramatist's "poetic physiognomy."

Introducing in this play what was to become a recurring structural feature in his writing, Abell places his barbed social satire within an unusual theatrical framework, steeped in the spirit of the ballet and the puppet stage. In the first of eleven scenes or "pictures," entitled "The Museum" and permeated with Abell's own experiences as an art student in Statens Museum for Kunst in the early twenties, the curtain rises to reveal an enormous picture, "painted in the conventional style of the fifteenth or sixteenth century," depicting Adam and Eve beneath a tree. On one side of the stage, an elaborately uniformed custodian is asleep; on the other, a tedious young man with pincenez sits studying his catalogue, pondering a reclining Venus. Slowly, in the spirit of magical ballets like "La Boutique fantasque," "Coppelia" or "Petruschka," the inanimate works of art in the drowsy museum come to life. Out of the orchestra pit emerges Kathrine of Lower Bavaria (catalogue number 408, "painted by unknown master, German school . . . hung in Rundenpfals Convent, removed in 1743"), a small, angular woman with yellowing cheeks, dressed in a fantastic Cranach headpiece and bearing her old-fashioned gilt frame. This busy comic manipulator, the highpoint of the Royal Theater production in Clara Pontoppidan's richly detailed interpretation, remains one of the most colorful of Abell's many vivid female characters. As she calls on Eve, the large Adam-and-Eve canvas is hoisted to reveal a paradisean garden of fantastic flowers and twining plants. Seated over tea in this paintbrush Eden, the two paintings gossip.

The mother of us all has been having domestic problems with Adam, who spends his time among the voluptuous and frolicsome females in the Rubens gallery. "I had rather hoped that some of the great religious pictures over in the cupola hall might have been able to talk some sense into him, but no," complains Eve, "after closing time they leave all their relics up in their frames and run around clowning on the floor."[27] This sort of Thornton Wilder whimsy is perishable, but before it begins to weary the principal intrigue is deftly set in motion. Discouraged with museum life, Eve is determined to escape into the real world; her fondest wish is to experience the "paradise" of childhood which she alone has been denied. Obligingly, the meddlesome Kathrine arranges the necessary miracle: Eve will, that very night, be born into the comfortable bourgeois home of the Ernst family on 14 Philistine Road (or "Jacob Ærekærsvej" in the untranslatable original!).

A series of fast-paced expressionistic scenes within this fantastic framework establish, with the adroit strokes of a Fritz Jürgensen cartoon (a comparison that occurred to more than one of the play's reviewers) or a clever advertising campaign, the second part of Abell's dialectical proposition. If the museum is in fact alive and quick with the zest of living, life itself is a dead museum of fossilized conventions and narcotizing traditions. A strident note that would soon become a dominant chord in Abell's writing, the selfish indifference of the myopic middle class toward the ominous events of the world around them, is sounded in the scene entitled "The Evening Paper." Grandfather, Aunt Anna, Aunt Missia, and Miss Funk are seated in disinterested comfort in their living room, and the impressionistic recital of catastrophes, epidemics, and revolutions with which the scene opens makes little impression on their trivial existence. "Thank goodness it's all so far away," is Aunt Anna's reaction—and one is reminded of the worker's angry speech to Edith in *The Melody that Got Lost:* "they duck into their goddam cream-colored washstand and slam the lid every time they hear a racket—and meantime the rest of us can lie around and crap out on the front page with big fat headlines and pictures of the deceased's sorrowing relatives."[28] Instead, the bourgeois family in *Eve* is far more concerned with the reported demise of "a man in Odense named Petersen," an event which gives rise to an exchange whose terrifying banality foreshadows the early absurd comedies of Ionesco:

AUNT ANNA. *(with lively interest)* Oscar Petersen? You don't mean to say Oscar Petersen?
GRANDFATHER.   That's right, a merchant named Oscar Petersen—did you know him?
AUNT ANNA. *(The following dialogue is fast and brisk)* Me?—No!—but I heard a lot about him from the Topps. They had some friends who used to know him—
MISS FUNK.   His wife was born Knudsen, I believe, couldn't that be right?
AUNT MISSIA.   Could very well be—she was probably a Knudsen from Bogense—

GRANDFATHER.   A daughter of the red-haired grocer Knudsen?— his
   sister was married to Uncle Jørgensen's partner—
AUNT MISSIA.   Was the daughter red-haired too, I wonder?
AUNT ANNA.   No, I think she was just plain blond—
MISS FUNK.   No, she was dark—chestnut brown—
GRANDFATHER.   Did you know her, Miss Funk?
MISS FUNK.   I wouldn't really say that—but I once had a dress altered by
   the same dressmaker—*(To Aunt Anna)* You know, the black one with the
   light front and the pleats in back—
AUNT ANNA.   Oh, that one?—was she good?—the dressmaker, I
   mean—because my patterned summer dress isn't a bit worn, but I cer-
   tainly can't use it the way it is. . . .

                                                                  (28–30)

   This "conversation" is interrupted by news that brother Ernst has
become a proud father. In a following scene (aptly titled
"Apotheosis") Grandfather's oration to an ornate pink cradle,
flanked by the parents and watched over by cardboard cutouts representing good fairies with wings and stars, outlines in a single
sentence the grim perimeters of the familial concentration camp in
which the impetuous Eve has been condemned to serve out her
childhood:

As the child's grandfather I would like to take the opportunity to wish that
the good old days may continue and that little Eve, should my son have no
male heirs, may grow up and find a nice, solid marriage with a man whose
name we can with pride and honor place after the company name with a
confidence-inspiring "and Co." (36)

The first repressive seasons of Eve's childhood pass in a theatrical
kaleidoscope of swift impressions, visually sustained in the original
production by the author's own witty and consciously "naive" settings and backdrops.[29] One of the play's most biting satirical
monologues is spoken by Eve's nurse (perfectly characterized by the
formidable Bodil Ipsen) to a painted cartoon of a parlormaid leaning
out a painted window. Spring turns to winter and back to summer
outside the Victorian villa on Philistine Road, rain falls from the
watering can of a cupid on a plywood cloud, the family ages before
the audience's eyes, Grandfather Ernst dies, and little Eve (who like
her mother Eline remains silent throughout the ordeal) is taught the
gentle but relentless tyranny of a "good upbringing" designed to

extinguish every flicker of personal self-expression. Thus, in a well-wrought scene entitled "Goblins," Eve, understandably frightened by a terrifying "children's story," is comforted by the mindless Aunt Anna with an arsenal of platitudes geared toward the restoration of "common sense":

... and besides, God watches over you—he sees everything and his eye never wanders from you—(whimper)—why of course angels exist—one always sits on your headboard while you're sleeping—tuck yourself in nicely now, you hear—my heavens, I have no idea whether angels wear overshoes—yes, perhaps they do—yes, naturally it's wet up there in the clouds—(whimper)—don't you worry about that at all, you just sleep—otherwise we'll be really angry at you and then we'll call the police and they'll come and get you—
(returns to the others and sits down)
That seemed to help—
(on the screen in the child's room an immense eye and angel wings are projected)
Now what's all this gossip about Mrs. Dustcastle? (52)

Perhaps the most harrowing "picture" in Eve's childhood album is the schoolroom sketch entitled "The World," a Strindbergian nightmare vision of the ceaseless repetition of absurd "truths." "The wickedest and sharpest of all the demonstrations of an outmoded upbringing," this scene, Schyberg declared, "should stand out as an exclamation mark in the text."[30] On a high dais sits the teacher, confronting a row of painted set pieces representing little girls at their desks; Eve takes her place on a line with these cutouts. "New pupils, always new pupils—I am the only one who remains. I and knowledge," intones the grotesque pedagogue. Pointer in hand, she strides to a gigantic two-dimensional globe:

SCHOOLTEACHER.   This, then, is the World. We shall come to what lies beyond it in religion class. The world is round and has these and those characteristics. The world looks thus and so. Repeat!!!
CHILDREN'S VOICES.   The world has these and those characteristics and looks thus and so!
SCHOOLTEACHER.   Many desire that it should look thus, and your parents would take you out of school if I told you it looked otherwise. It *must* look thus, for otherwise I would risk dismissal. From the beginning!!!

CHILDREN'S VOICES.   The world has these and those characteristics and looks thus and so! We don't care either, because the Carlsens are giving a dance on Saturday and then we'll dance with boys.
SCHOOLTEACHER.   Only when the world is thus and is perceived as such is it worth living in. Fortunately we live in the most enlightened period in history. You are to hate anyone who says the opposite. What is more, we have very definite lists of what you must hate and what you must admire. Everything is right there in the Rules. Repeat!!!
CHILDREN'S VOICES.   We repeat—we repeat—we don't care. We can always memorize—we repeat—we repeat—we don't care. We can always memorize—(*The murmur of children's voices continues as the curtain falls.*)

(56–57)

As these samples indicate, Abell's humor in these childhood scenes is broad, articulately black, but ultimately more playful than passionate. "He is no Bert Brecht mercilessly swinging his satirical lash to all sides," remarked critic Georg Wiinblad. "He is rather like an intelligent little boy playing puppet theater, working with paper dolls, painted set pieces, and all sorts of scene changes and fly-gallery mechanics that become transformed into ideas, symbols, and allegories."[31] "One is not caught up in the fate of his characters or in the action, but only in what *he* will think of next," added Svend Borberg in his review. "It is too early to illustrate an idea before that idea has been fully thought through. . . . *Eve* is to a certain extent merely a series of illustrations for a work of *art* which he has *not* written."[32]

The play's tone and direction change abruptly, moreover, in the last three scenes of its long first act, as the author finds himself in the throes of pointing the predictable moral of his allegorical satire. Abandoning both the taut expressionistic style of the earlier scenes and the device of a silent and passive child-victim, he reintroduces the mature Eve as an active dramatic character. Her conditioning completed, she emerges from the schoolroom setting to enter, under the ever-watchful eyes of the spying aunts, an ad man's cartoon of a fashionable seaside resort (a mermaid sits reading a cheap pulp novel beside painted, two-dimensional sand dunes and has lines like: "Thank Neptune I'm only human to the waist"!). Superficially liberated and "modern" in her views, she quarrels fiercely with a would-be conquest who, like the audience, easily detects the

Ernst mentality not far beneath her unconventional facade. "Let anyone just scratch the least bit in your polished surface and the aunts shine through," the young man tells her bluntly. Despite her modernized appearance, her family has succeeded in molding a thoroughly materialistic and predictably dull pillar of bourgeois society in its own image. "You were born in a museum and, just wait, *that's* where you'll stay," he predicts with unconscious irony (67). Having served her childhood, Eve is destined for "a nicely furnished marriage" designed to perpetuate the deadly pattern.

Following a prolonged expositional scene which returns to the museum in order to depict Adam's drunken return from the delights of the Rubens room and his subsequently sobered and conscience-stricken determination to rescue Eve from the predicament in which Kathrine's scheme has unwittingly placed her, the play moves toward a turning point. Dressed in her wedding gown and already preparing to change clothes for her honeymoon, Eve is suddenly brought to her senses by the sight of a bouquet of roses accompanied by a terse I-told-you-so card from the prophetic young man on the beach. Characteristically, however, Abell solves the dramatic problem of a convincing anagnorisis by substituting a visual *coup de théâtre*. Eve comes to no effective realization of her own, nor is she aided by her apparently mute mother Eline. Instead, as she sits staring into space oblivious to the sounds of the wedding party outside, a shadow passes in the moonlight, the door to the garden opens, and Adam emerges to carry her, still in her bridal gown and shouting with delight, back to their painted paradise.

Had the play ended here, as well it might, it would have carried its point no further than was the case in *The Melody that Got Lost*. Both Eve and Larsen lose touch with their life-giving origins, nearly succumb to the stultifying effects of middle-class conventionality, and are finally extricated from their difficulties by a more actively energetic spouse. In Larsen's case, we are asked to believe in a hypothetical solution to a problem that in fact remains unresolved. In Eve's case, however, the playwright does attempt—with mixed success—to precipitate a confrontation with the source of the problem, in an extraordinary second act that returns to the museum for the trial of "Eve vs. her family." Although Schyberg calls this long, disquisitory sequence "the play's Achilles heel," later critics such as Svend Erichsen have disagreed: "In none of his other plays does the political and intellectual center of gravity rest so decidedly and triumphantly in the last act."[33] One is far less swayed by the trial scene's very modest intellectual or political ballast, however, than by the uninhibited theatrical exuberance with which Abell keeps it from drowning in talk.

The chief source of energy is Adam who, after vigorously deposing the museum's director, sends Kathrine in search of suitable paintings to form a court which will sit in judgment on the family's offence. When the aunts, the deaf Miss Funk, Ernst, and the silent Eline appear in quest of the missing bride, the scene is suddenly transformed into a vast hall of pictures, "all the faces of which appear like spectators in a courtroom" (98). A high judges' bench is rolled in from the background, and seats for the witnesses, the prosecution, and the defense are carried in by extras dressed in gaudy historical costumes. When the astonished Ernst family has been ordered into the dock, the "judges"—paintings conveniently possessing wigs—enter, and the "jury"—a museumlike row of white marble busts—is convened. Adam, determined to convict the Ernsts of utterly distorting Eve's personality, has reserved the role of prosecutor for himself. Gravely demanding a plea from the unwilling defendants, the presiding judge (played with appropriate weightiness by Johannes Poulsen) describes the charge:

that the family, partly with intent, partly unconsciously in connection with a well-planned scheme, did lead the child along a very definite path, in such a way that the end result would inevitably be to the benefit of the family itself or the family's own ideals. Have people the right to regard their offspring as a piece of personal property, serving their own interests? Have people the right to make plans far into the future on their children's behalf, and, thanks to habit, to bind them to such an extent that they at last don't know whether they are seeing with their own eyes or with someone else's, if in fact they even see at all? The prosecution thinks not, and asks the court to judge and judge severely. . . . (104–5)

Though the outcome of the case of "Eve vs. her family" is, in Abell's ideology, a foregone conclusion, the playwright earns his unmitigated verdict of guilty through an effective deployment of dramatic surprises.

The first and certainly the most surprising witness for the prosecution is the upholstered and tassled armchair which has stood as a mute onlooker in the Ernst family parlor. To coax the reticent chair

into speech, Adam arranges the stage, in almost Pirandellian fashion, with the familiar properties and furnishings of the bourgeois
living room on Philistine Road. Above the low walls of the room, the
judges' bench and museum surroundings remain discernible, rein-
forcing in visual terms the play's controlling frame image. Thus
conjured, the armchair begins (in the guise of a figure who emerges
from behind it "clad in the chair's brocade and upholstered and
decorated with tassles and fringes" and sits with crossed legs) its
ringing denunciation of the life-dispossessing atmosphere generated
in this "battleground" of domestic repressiveness:

THE CHAIR.   This is a world picture—a fortified world picture. The
    well-kept garden just outside the windows is cross-hatched with invisible
    trenches, and the nice parlor table right across from me knows from
    experience what it means to be used as a barricade—
ADAM.   But what are they fighting for?
THE CHAIR.   For the right to keep the past . . . the only thing that can
    disturb their peace is the future—the future is the enemy—it goes by on
    the sidewalk outside, it lurks along the newly painted picket-fence and
    threatens to seep in if we don't seal all the house's pores in time and put
    double padlocks on the attic rooms. . . . Eve was planned and trained so
    she could serve as an insurance against the future they feared—if you
    don't believe me, just ask the walls, the table, the pictures, the lamp—
    we're all prisoners in this room, just like Eve—
        (asks)
    Isn't it true what I say?
VOICES.   Yes!
THE CHAIR.   Haven't we all seen how she was slowly conditioned, on the
    pretext that it was for her own good?
VOICES.   Yes!
THE CHAIR.   And was it for her own good?
VOICES.   They said it was!!!

                                                            (110–12)

Involuntarily, the family members themselves are hypnotically
drawn, like Pirandello's six characters, into Adam's parlor-theater to
replay bits of their lives that corroborate the armchair's damning
testimony. Aunt Missia's pitiful "love affair"—a single afternoon in
the park—was skilfully terminated by the family's loving tyranny:

If only you had forbidden it, I might have pulled myself together and dared
anyway. But you just spoke kindly and understandingly and gave good

advice and quite casually mentioned something about gratitude.—You go right ahead and impose a debt on us, but you say nothing about its having to be repaid someday. Suddenly one bright day you stand there, demanding that we hand over our future—and it's exactly the same thing you're trying to do to Eve. (114–15)

Eline, who suddenly breaks her silence for the first time in the play, confesses that she has been Eve's mute ally, trying to "help her by concealing certain things from her father and making sure that, by various excuses, she had as much freedom as possible"—but she has recognized too late her timid failure as a mother and her powerlessness as a woman to overcome the "sea of sensible arguments and logical explanations that men come up with whenever they must be right at any cost" (p. 119). These brief glimmers of self-knowledge are fleeting, however, and the family soon subsides again into the unconcerned oblivion of its "velvet fortress" existence, epitomized by the selfish and overbearing Aunt Anna's abiding interest in poached eggs and burnt almonds. "The great passions," warned the armchair earlier, "are securely locked up in the bookcase where they stand side by side with God the Almighty, Creator of heaven and earth, who must also resign himself to being an illustration in a book" (109).

Potentially the most dramatic surprise in this act is Eve's unexpected assumption of the role of defense counsel; the prospect of a Shavian duel of ideas never materializes, however, for Abell lacks Shaw's unique ability to generate comic conflict by endowing each character-ideologue in a discussion play with equal articulateness and force. Eve's plea for mercy rests on her unconvincing attempt to shift the focus of the trial, by developing her metaphor of childhood as a kind of universal military service ("no one is deferred, all medical excuses are invalid, the tour of duty is long and for many quite onerous"[34]) whose ills are inevitable and whose systematized taboos can be traced back through the ages to Adam and herself: "The actions of those accused were dictated by their past, their milieu, and their social class—by everything that surrounds them—and this is where the charge ought to have been laid. This is where I wish it had been laid, because then I would never in the world have stood before this court as defense counsel" (126).

Dramaturgically speaking, however, Eve makes a sound point here. Abell's unsavage satire pokes fun at befuddled, comic-strip extensions of a (purportedly) pernicious social class, but it never presents a serious threat to the underpinnings of the class itself. Beneath this reluctance may perhaps be seen that personal artistic "doubleness" to which Abell's contemporaries have so often referred: "He attacked the middle class, but was firmly anchored to its life style. He was its victim. It was his prison, and he never escaped from it. I think he realized it himself."[35] In this play, the dramatic resolution is, quite literally, provided by a *deus ex machina* which—used without any of Brecht's trenchant irony in, for example, *The Threepenny Opera*—attaches an acceptable "theater" solution to the fundamentally unresolved dramatic conflict. After the "jury" of marble busts has unaccountably shattered itself to bits in its efforts to reach a verdict, the court is obliged to place itself in the hands of an "impartial judge"—a painter who has been following the proceedings from the rafters and who now descends on his scaffold to rule on the outcome of the trial.

This felicitously working-class representative of the "real" world beyond the museum (acted by the play's director Holger Gabrielsen) is the dramatic cousin of the worker who comes to Edith's aid in *The Melody that Got Lost*. In *Eve* he pronounces both the trial's verdict and its moral: the Ernst family is "condemned" to remain forever in the museum as a lifeless family portrait (a mild fate, in that they will fail even to notice the difference!) while Adam and Eve are sentenced to return, "without baggage," to the world outside, to view life with fresh, "surprised" eyes and to teach others to call things by whatever new names they please. For, as the playwright's spokesman adds, "the world is no museum. It's as fresh and new each day as when Adam first saw a hen lay an egg—though there are some who take hold of it with old hands—and it doesn't like that, no matter how neatly it's done" (123). The curtain falls on the Ernst family portrait, the departing workman's song of freedom, and Kathrine of Lower Bavaria's farewell to Adam and Eve ("there are, after all, quite a few of us who belong in the museum—I've discovered that, and besides I have such a hard time remembering new names"), but the ending remains an ambiguous beginning intended, it would seem, to prod each spectator into creating his own solution. The aim of Kjeld Abell's theater, Schyberg observes in his illuminating study of the dramatist, "is in no sense primarily to provide answers but to raise questions, to present problems and suggest possibilities—above all not to soothe and satisfy, but to activate the audience into direct and personal co-authorship and co-creation."[36] This conscious attempt to engage the audience's participatory imagination represents one of the most characteristic features of Abell's dramaturgy.

As many of its first reviewers remarked, *Eve Serves Her Childhood* held no thematic surprises for audiences already familiar with "The Widow in the Mirror" and *The Melody that Got Lost*. The tension between the "open" and the "closed" individual, between a free and open response to life's potentialities and a waxworks existence circumscribed by dead conventions and traditions, had already become—and would remain—a persistent Abellian leitmotiv. However, in terms of form this play represents a far more finished and substantial work, much less bound to the specific zeitgeist of the thirties, than *Melody*, and it marks a convincing step forward toward its author's goal of a theater which "should always be the free imagination's fantastic sanctuary."[37] Control continued to present a problem: "Kjeld Abell can do many things. He can also babble on a little too long about things that could be said a little more briefly," Schyberg noted in his review, while Svend Borberg added that his own heady prescription for a retheatricalized "theater of revelations" seemed almost to be taken too literally by Abell in his eagerness to experiment. Nevertheless, as Harald Engberg observed in a memorial essay written after the playwright's death, it is basically "foolish to demonstrate the looseness of his construction: this is what determines the dancing quality of his art, whose point of departure is the ballet. He is almost always more interesting in his structural flaws than others are in their solidity."[38]

Performed forty-one times in repertory during the Royal Theater's 1936–1937 season and subsequently revived from time to time elsewhere, *Eve Serves Her Childhood* remains among the wittiest and most relevant of Abell's plays. In one sense, it represents a cul-de-sac in his development, a festive fusillade of baroque humor not repeated in the series of darker and more serious dramas that follow. In another sense, however, the satirical tone and burlesque techniques which characterize this play do continue to permeate a rather neglected but not insignificant part of Abell's production—the revues and sketches which he contributed, often in collaboration with Poul Henningsen, around 1940, and which may be seen as belonging to a continuous Danish tradition of revue and cabaret theater.

IV   Satirical Revues (1937–1940)

The lively tradition of the satirical revue in Denmark, reaching back to the nineteenth-century vaudevilles of J. L. Heiberg, with their crisp comic dialogue and polemical and topical songs, and extending to contemporary experiments in the revue genre by such playwrights as Klaus Rifbjerg and Ernst Bruun Olsen, drew renewed vigor during the late twenties and early thirties from the efforts of the gifted architect, designer, and lyricist Poul Henningsen. Determined to provide an alternative to the taste for spectacular musicals and lavish operettas, the versatile "P. H." sought to reintroduce a simpler cabaret form, a more intimate platform style focusing on witty song texts and satirical monologues. Abell's first two plays had left no doubt about his abilities as a writer of satirical sketches, and in *Mars på Weekend* (*Mars Takes a Holiday*), a short revue-comedy produced at Riddersalen at the close of 1937, his few contributions added a new poetic dimension to the conventional revue format. Collaborating for the first time with Henningsen and Mogens Dam, Abell furnished a characteristic mythological framework for the proceedings—Mars, god of war, is weary of the pressures of the times and decides to take a "quiet" weekend holiday in peaceful Denmark—but his most notable contribution to the production was a stinging caricature of the Danish film industry, tailored to the talents of the unsurpassed revue comedienne Liva Weel. "It is the poets whom we have hitherto been lacking as contributors to our revues," wrote an effusive Frederik Schyberg in *Politiken* (December 27, 1937). "They can perhaps not write revues themselves, but they can breathe life into them, exactly as Kjeld Abell did last evening."

In his *Askepot—og dog* (*Cinderella—and yet*), a light revue comedy in fifteen scenes produced at the Apollo Theater in February 1939, Abell made a more extended—though not wholly successful—effort to conquer the popular revue stage. The strength of this production lay, characteristically, in a theatrical flair inherent in the playwright's approach, and shared by a cast headed by such fine variety performers as Marguerite Viby and Hans W. Petersen. "All that was in him of theater, *petit guignol*, pantomime, fly-gallery, and set pieces found expression," Poul Henningsen later recalled.[39] The target of the revue's entertaining but unsavage satire was the radio, a recurrent preoccupation in Abell's work. His Cinderella is a girl who is determined to appear on the radio; her Prince Charming is a somewhat disreputable playwright whose heart she softens! "He taught us," declared Hans Brix with his carefully calculated innocence, "that happiness consists not of wealth but a happy heart, and that [the Copenhagen] Tivoli is paint and canvas and a trinket shop, and that the radio is a magnified Tivoli, just as phony but all year round. We must stick to the commonplace and just be natural."[40]

Of rather more interest is *Guderne te'r sig (The Gods Carry On)*, a much less conventional revue experiment created for the Apollo Theater by Abell and Henningsen in September 1940. Enjoying only a shortened two-week run because of the censorship problems imposed by the German occupation, this mythological fantasy was a spirited modernization of Holberg's eighteenth-century "philosophical comedy" *Plutus, or The Trial between Poverty and Wealth* (1751)—itself an elaborate scenic spectacle based on Aristophanes's last play, and filled with splendid processions, magnificent costumes, special lighting effects, and gods in flying machines. In his free updating of Aristophanes and Holberg, Abell created an ironic fable that was far closer to the wry theater parables of Giraudoux than to the conventions of a standard Apollo revue. The mythic conflict between Plutus, god of wealth, and Penia, goddess of frugality, held promising topical relevance during the months following the German invasion. "Frugality is the order of the day," wrote Schyberg in his review, "and hence Penia's role has been expanded so that it is now *she* around whom the action revolves."[41] The goddess of frugality, after a brief youthful affair with Plutus that resulted in the birth of their daughter Wantonia ("for when wealth and poverty meet . . " etc.), is now his enemy and pines in exile. The god of gold, his sight restored by the citizens of Athens who thereby hope to ensure that his gifts are distributed to "the right ones," sees, all too clearly, the greed and corruption beneath the respectable faces. He distributes accordingly, and bitter envy is the result—the Malcontents, conspiring in masks and capes in the Athenian night, form a party and adopt a telling slogan: "Down with the others. Up with us!" At last, Plutus wearily begs Jupiter to restore his blindness, and Penia regains her rightful ascendancy. Sam Besekow's direction and Svend Johansen's rich and witty designs for a festively theatrical Athens provided Henningsen and Abell's comedy with a framework that might, Schyberg was convinced, have otherwise attracted international notice "if we were not living in a closed world." Under the circumstances, however, the lavish production soon closed, and no manuscript has survived.

In striking contrast, Abell's earlier two-act revue *Dyveke*, which opened at Riddersalen only a few weeks after the German invasion on April 9, 1940, achieved an astonishing run of more than 400 performances. Three key elements contributed to the success: Abell's text, which represents his best revue comedy and is the only one to have been published, Poul Henningsen's songs, and the impressive performance of Liva Weel, to whom the play was tailored. *Dyveke* is a mixture of light musical comedy, farce, and rather academic literary parody—and it thus comes as no surprise to learn that Abell had already completed an early draft of the work during his student days at the University of Copenhagen. This "modern Capriccio on an ancient theme" (to borrow one reviewer's apt phrase) is a comic reassessment of the traditional character of Dyveke, mistress of the medieval king Christjern the Second, as she has been conventionally depicted in Danish literature—that is, the gentle, self-sacrificing heroine of O. J. Samsøe's sentimental tragedy *Dyveke* (1796), the romantic suicide of Carsten Hauch's mock autobiography *Vilhelm Zabern* (1834), the proud, plucky woman of the people of H. C. Andersen's *Dreams of the King* (1844), the idealized spirit of Holger Drachmann's "Dyveke-Sange," set to music in Peter Heise's characteristic *romance* idiom, or the mild, poetic victim of Kaj Munk's modern pastiche *The Dictatress* (1938). Nothing in all this represents the truth, insists the "real" Dyveke of Abell's comedy, a vigorous, saucy Renaissance realist determined to correct the misinformation about her being spread by the excessively "delicate and sensitive" muses:

the only damn thing they ever in their whole lives have treated lightly is the truth—they come fluttering and flying and settle sweetly on poets' shoulders and whisper a lot of sweet bunk in their ears. But they forget to tell how we really were—that we drank a couple of tankards of ale every day, ate with our fingers. . . .

Everybody says they know me, either from Kaj Munk or Heise—but if anyone dares to mention Heise just once more, I'll start swinging—I hate concerts—give me a couple of punches in the nose in a dark alley with a crossdraught rather than two tickets to Carnegie Hall any day. . . .[42]

This theme—the unequal struggle of the "true" personality against a conventional, superimposed image which the world prefers to regard as "real"—has its serious, Pirandellian possibilities, but Abell prefers to ignore them and adheres instead to an amusing topsyturvydom. Dyveke, who (like Eve) is helped to escape from her heavenly museum, becomes embroiled with a modern poet engaged in writing a Dyveke film. She soon finds herself in a mental home, is ultimately tracked down by the muses with the aid of King Christjern ("he works like a seismograph—if Dyveke is within a certain radius, he registers earthquake"!), and reascends to heaven at last after having shattered the false image of her that had persisted. *Dyveke*, the last and most accomplished of Abell's revues, is far more than just a skilfully wrought frame on which to hang a dozen of Poul Henningsen's cleverest lyrics. It sustains an articulate comic vision, and succeeds in attaining artistic unity. "Abell's Capriccio cavorts over the stage like a song, a dance, a game," Schyberg declared in *Politiken* (June 1, 1940). "So light, so outspoken, so free, so charming, this play, which balances on the edge of student burlesque without being a revue, is a bagatelle that is elevated to something close to poetry."

By the time this light-hearted satirical revue was staged, however, two new serious plays by Abell—*Anna Sophie Hedvig* and *Judith*—had already appeared at the Royal Theater, and had profoundly altered the shape of the playwright's poetic physiognomy. His revues, interesting chiefly as indicators of certain continuing thematic and stylistic traits, round off the series of social comedies and satires with which he occupied himself during the thirties. In general, this group of plays comprises the first face of Abell's dramaturgy, hallmarked by his youthful revolt against that stifling bourgeois conventionality which Dyveke succinctly characterizes as "the thousand tiny threads of custom" that "binds us hand and mouth." As the thirties passed and the decade's troubled economic situation was overshadowed by the threat and swift reality of Nazi aggression, Abell's posture as an artist altered. The verbal arabesques and pirouettes of the comedies (themselves never completely apolitical) gave way to a new tone and a new form. In *Anna Sophie Hedvig*, the first and most popular example of this new direction in his work, Abell turns from the ridicule of social customs and conventions to a more comprehensive and passionate rejection of political passivity and apathy in the face of tyranny. Running through this second group of wartime plays is the theme so forcefully expressed by Delescluze's words in Nordahl Grieg's *The*

Defeat, a drama of political resistance which had a stunning impact on Abell and his contemporaries when first acted in Copenhagen in 1937: "We have learned the bitter truth that good can only survive through force."

CHAPTER 3

Political Drama

I Anna Sophie Hedvig (1939)

THE political apathy and indifference of the self-centered middle class, already a target area in Abell's earlier social plays and revues, emerges as a major thematic concern in the cycle of plays which deal, more or less explicitly, with the threat to personal freedom posed by the rise and spread of Nazi aggression. Although these "political" dramas continue to be animated by the persistent Abellian conflict between the "open" and the "closed" individual—the struggle of life against its nullification by false values and inhibiting societal pressures—the elements of action in them are more dramatically concrete than in the earlier comic fantasies. Concomitantly, the focus of concern shifts from the social mass to the individual and the affirmative, existential action which is required of him in the face of tyranny.

After more than two years of relative silence, during which he produced only the ballet scenario for "Thorvaldsen" and an adaptation of Oliver Twist for the Danish School Theater (Skolescenen), Abell returned to the Royal Theater stage on New Year's Day 1939 with his three-act drama Anna Sophie Hedvig. The strongly acted production, directed by Holger Gabrielsen and remembered for Clara Pontoppidan's vivid portrayal of the title character, was in itself a significant factor in the wide popular acceptance of what remains Abell's best known work. However, the full explanation of the play's remarkable contemporary impact is to be found in its underlying message of political resistance—an exhortation readily apprehended by audiences living in the growing shadow of the Third Reich. In numerous articles and speeches from the thirties, Abell had urgently warned those "who let themselves be impressed by the elimination of unemployment in Hitler's Germany and the punctuality of train departures in Mussolini's Italy" to recognize the dangers of fascism. "Termite dwellings spring up like mountains with cannon embrasures. Termite armies march in regulated ranks and with an impressive step that lets itself be photographed in all the world's newspapers," he wrote with bitter irony in a 1938 article called "Spring in Europe." "We are all destined to be termites—and whether we like it or not makes no difference at all."[1] *Anna Sophie Hedvig*, however, is far from being a shrill antifascist *lehrstück*. "Theater as direct propaganda holds no interest," Abell reminds us, for "propaganda must be made adroitly, it must be wrapped up so that the work of the audience becomes to unwrap it."[2] The character of Anna Sophie Hedvig, the mild little spinster schoolteacher who takes action to rid her small world of evil, became a symbol of freedom, capable of speaking more forcefully to the dramatist's contemporaries than any political tract could do. So forcefully, in fact, that discussions of the play's theme and ideas have virtually overwhelmed attempts to examine dispassionately its incontrovertible structural weaknesses.

Abell's principal weapons in this drama are a strong situation (almost melodramatically so) and the venerable but serviceable device of a dramatic catalyst introduced into a potentially explosive situation. In the glittering midst of one of his stuffiest and most shallow-spirited families, the playwright places his grey, self-effacing, and apparently harmless heroine—an unexpected house guest who has inexplicably deserted her post at a provincial girls' school and now finds herself a superfluous and barely welcome participant in a business dinner of crucial importance for the family's economy. The complacent after-dinner conversation, replete with Abell's customary satirical barbs and deliberate banalities, drifts to the justification of taking another's life. As the company smugly agrees that no "enlightened, cultivated, modern individual" could ever kill, the hitherto silent schoolteacher quietly casts her dramatic bombshell. Confronted in her own school-world with the rise of a malicious and implacably power-mad tyrant bent on seizing the principalship from a better qualified but less aggressive rival, Anna Sophie Hedvig has taken justice upon herself and has murdered the noxious Mrs. Miller by throwing her down a flight of stairs:

It was as though I suddenly saw from my little world into the big one—the world of the newspapers—the one we hear about, and talk about, but which is so far away. The world where it is not murder to take a life. Where an individual's opinion must be shared by everyone else. She was going to destroy my world. Didn't I have to defend it before she attacked? Must we not defend our little worlds? Is it not they which together make up the big one?[3]

Clearly, Abell has serious designs on us here. His play is a protest against passive humanism and political neutrality, an allegorical attack on all those who, in the words of John, the radical young son of the household, "are neither for nor against but always in between": "We always understand both sides of a question. That's our glaring weakness in relation to the others who insist on getting their way, without any in-betweens. They drive straight ahead—and we give up and make the excuse that we're too humane" (62). People must, according to the play's tough-minded morality, take a stand concerning the world around them, and must bear full responsibility for that stand. We remain free and alive only through engagement and direct action, and thus Anna Sophie Hedvig's decision to destroy tyranny is an "heroic" reaffirmation of her existence. "At times it may make perfect sense, may even be mandatory, to act, to kill, and to die for what one believes is right," Schyberg declares in his glowing review of the first production. "Only in this way is it possible for the world to become better one day."[4]

There is little in Abell's philosophic melodrama (to borrow Eric Bentley's description of Sartre's drama[5]) to astonish those who know their French existential playwrights—or even those who recall Irwin Shaw's popular antifascist allegory, *The Gentle People,* produced by the Group Theater in the same year.[6] The idea that the meek must eventually stand up to the bullies if they ever hope to inherit the earth is a familiar one in the drama of this period. However, the transparency of the ethical stance in Abell's play— rendered even clearer and less ambiguous by Schyberg's influential review—has perhaps tended to divert attention from the curious discrepancy that exists between the strength and aggressiveness of the theme and the oblique and even evasive manner in which it is dramatized. "How," demanded Hans Brix in a terse, disgruntled review that nicely counterbalances Schyberg's panegyric, "can a playwright imagine he can defend direct action by tiptoeing on indirect stocking-feet?"[7] Brix's shrewd objections, shared by various other reviewers, address themselves primarily to problems of dramatic form, and it is here—in the play's structural fabric—that its vulnerability mainly lies.

Anna Sophie Hedvig represents an obvious and deliberate departure from Abell's earlier expressionist techniques. "This is again a new form I am trying," he told an interviewer before the premiere, "not because I have shelved the old one, with which I will continue to work, but because it seems that the subject itself, Anna Sophie Hedvig, demands its *own* special form." In replacing the "dramatic narrative of *Melody* and *Eve*" with "dramatic action," he has turned to "an *apparently* old-fashioned form." "The realism which the play contains is born of the times," the playwright concludes rather cryptically.[8] In fact, however, the "realistic" texture of the play is only skin deep, and its use of the familiar devices of the drawing-room play and the thriller is freely combined with a distinctly cinematic fluidity of time and place. (Abell, it should be noted, had already completed the first of several film scripts, "Millionærdrengen" ["The Rich Boy"] in 1936.) The main action—Anna Sophie Hedvig's arrival, her revelation, and its shattering effect on the dinner party—is precariously poised within a double framework. On one level, the entire play is a flashback, a suspense story that is "narrated" by the maid to two young people who mistakenly stumble into the darkened apartment some hours after the fateful party has disbanded and the schoolteacher has been taken into custody. Though Brix certainly goes too far in asserting that "on the stage time cannot roll backwards," it is nonetheless difficult to refute his contention that this narrative framework—intended though it may be to establish a mood of suspenseful gloom, to provide perspective and contrast, or to explain the power failure which will conveniently intervene in the main action—is essentially unrelated and hence misleading. The play's second, broader frame, far more thematically integrated and completely nonrealistic, represents "the big world of the newspapers"—where men struggle actively and courageously for their beliefs, and to which Anna Sophie Hedvig's action is ultimately related. A doomed prisoner, suggesting a soldier from the Spanish civil war, is twice shown standing impassively against a wall, waiting to be executed. At the end of the play, the timid schoolteacher places herself and her deed beside the condemned soldier, and symbolically shares his fate at the hands of the firing squad.

Within this double framework, the story of Anna Sophie Hedvig's strange visit and its consequences unfolds in an almost filmic manner, depicted in a fairly symmetrical sequence of episodes which dissolve, one into the next, by means of a "cross fade" technique ("the light fades, the stage is dark for a moment, and a clock is heard striking seven; when the light returns, the room is in evening light, the drapes are closed, the lamps are lighted . . ."). In one of its dimensions, to which six of these episodes are devoted, the play focuses on the apathetic middle-class milieu in which the schoolteacher's astonishing revelation causes turmoil and domestic chaos. Her only defender, the young radical John ("the usual type with jazz records and Bach and slightly negative opinions about everything") is alone in recognizing the justification and importance of her spontaneous act. As he goes on to unmask the hypocrisy and indifference of the family's so-called neutrality ("we have taken a stand by taking no stand"), his denunciations of the family's bourgeois values bring his mother to acknowledge the falsity of her own position: "I felt more and more like a mere ornament—a frivolous, grinning ornament on a business. The business was the main thing—finally for me too. I no longer existed—just as Anna Sophie Hedvig didn't—I was embalmed in my habits" (71). With disastrous results for his father's business interests, John also challenges the honesty of the dangerous and crafty capitalist Hoff, the dinner guest who cynically hands the visitor over to the authorities. As the domestic crisis reaches its climax, the Father, deserted by his wife and faced with ruin at Hoff's hands, declares wearily: "I have no need to see my defeat clearer than now. I thought—no, I don't think anything. We sat here in judgment over Anna Sophie Hedvig's fate—but she has judged ours. Maybe it was something that had to be done—now it is done" (72).

This statement's rhetorical ring of conclusiveness notwithstanding, however, Anna Sophie Hedvig's "bombshell" remains, in a dramatic sense, a theoretical construct, inconclusively related to the drawing-room types who quarrel over her fate. No one within this dimension of the play is directly implicated in her life, and throughout the main conflict she remains apart and virtually silent. The philosophic defense of her standpoint is left to John, the playwright's angry spokesman, and, though his arguments cause dramatic sparks to fly, we are continually *told* rather than *shown* why and how this sudden encounter with naked, passionate commitment to a course of action will reshape the family's destiny. There is, in other words, a curious disconnectedness between Anna Sophie Hedvig's unseen deed and its postulated effect upon the uninvolved middle-class environment to which it is made known.

Another level of action in the play (the fourth, if we count the two framing actions and the main action of the dinner party itself) takes place in the past tense, in two "flashbacks within the flashback" that return, in the midst of the dinner party, to the night of Mrs. Miller's murder in a deserted provincial school. In the first of these essentially expository scenes, a vignette rich in Abell's special brand of family satire, the janitor and his wife hear a scream and discover the body; a subsequent episode affords Anna Sophie Hedvig the opportunity to explain the morality of her action to Ester, the schoolgirl who enables her to escape detection: "It's not enough to be 'all right,' Ester. That's just about the worst thing one can be. The others fight with entirely different weapons—and all the time you sit there and are just 'all right.' And for whose benefit? Only one's own conscience. Do we have the right? And meanwhile our world is destroyed" (50). The keenly sensed night atmosphere of the empty school building—freshly varnished floors and an air filled with "vengeful beings" ("all those whom the teachers interpret and explain—all the great ones" who rage "like stormwinds through the classrooms" when school is out)—is poetically alive with Abell's own childhood memories as a schoolmaster's son.[9] Characteristically, meanwhile, the playwright draws back from dramatizing the actual confrontation between his protagonist and her shadowy opponent, whose destructive malice is never shown and who thus remains, in Schyberg's terms, "only a symbol of greater and more dangerous concepts." But can a murder which is made the dramatic crux of an apparently realistic "mystery" play be handled in purely poetic or "symbolic" fashion? The circumvention of an "obligatory" scene showing the principals in the conflict "in an intellectual hand-to-hand struggle" convinced Brix that these school flashbacks "fizzle out in discussions about the event and in a little atmospheric mystification that sends no chills whatsoever down our spine." Schyberg's review, intent above all else on articulating the more universal political aspects of the play's theme, takes the opposite tack, insisting that Abell is in fact not concerned with the event itself but "with its effects, its philosophic effects, on the minds of the audience, and its tangible effects on the individuals on the stage who listen to Anna Sophie Hedvig's story." "Sometimes," this writer adds later in his little book about the dramatist:

he simply *states* his meaning, without showing and *proving* it to us. This hangs together with the nature of his talent, an aptitude or a shortcoming but at the same time a conviction with him, an influence from the French theater, which has always been a word-theater more than an action-theater and of which Kjeld Abell is the only typical example in Danish literature.[10]

Brix, however, steals the final, persuasively passionate word in this imaginary little debate between the period's two most perceptive drama critics: "Theater is word *and* action, not words about action. The action and the word must be inextricably bound together, the idea must spring from the word and release itself in action. And the poet's genius can not be a polite and cautious schoolmistress on Thanksgiving vacation in the big city. Tear the soul out of people, that's drama."

This clash of critical views in a sense epitomizes the wider and sometimes acrimonious disagreement which Abell's untraditional methods often seem to have engendered. Both critics are, to an extent, right about *Anna Sophie Hedvig*. It is, as one of its characters remarks in retrospect, "no tragedy"—and its meandering structure often vitiates the full force of its strong central idea. Abell's meek, anti-heroic heroine provokes none of the fiercely emotional "soul tearing" caused by such modern dramatic intruders as O'Neill's Hickey, Williams' Blanche DuBois, or Dürrenmatt's Claire Zachanassian. Nor, of course, has the playwright meant that she should do so. Through most of the play, her character seems strangely distant and peripheral, an idea more than a living human being. However, her final long speech, delivered in the closing moments as she quietly joins the condemned man in the prison yard, marks a bold dramatic peripety, a moving existential reaffirmation that at last fuses philosophy and emotion and places both the speaker and her symbolic act in a universal perspective:

There are so many who die—so terribly many who die for something without ever really knowing why. I wouldn't know either, if someone suddenly stood me up against a wall. I wouldn't be able to explain it. It's something you feel—something you fully and completely believe—isn't it wonderful that existence, no matter how it may look, can still get someone to die for it.

It's as though you face death in order to live. Your faith keeps the world alive, and makes it seem just as young as it ever was.[11] You don't sit by and satisfy yourselves with the thought that a time will come someday when it will be wrong to kill, when no one will have to die for others, or believe blindly without knowing why. You fight for that future—when you die, it is to make it possible. You do not say that it is no use—you know it is some use. . . .[12] (79–80)

The light dims and picks out the smiling faces of Anna Sophie Hedvig and the prisoner, faint drums grow suddenly louder, in the darkness the firing squad's salvo is heard. Only then does Abell's indictment of the aggressors who ravage the earth—the petty tyrants like Mrs. Miller, the exploiters like Hoff, and, behind them all, Hitler himself, the ominous unnamed voice on the radio "that we should have strangled before he got so far" (64)—reach its full dramatic articulation. For the impressive revival of the play in February 1957, the author made several cuts in this last speech to modify its political, utopian overtones and tighten its personal and tragic focus on the speaker herself.[13] On the stage this character, given the powers of an actress like Clara Pontoppidan, springs to life and provides a controlling force that unifies the play's disparate levels of action. No clear or unambiguous conclusion is reached, however, for Abell's theater, in this work as elsewhere, builds on questions rather than certainties. "If the poet answers, thinks he answers, his answer is a thousand questions. The answer comes from the auditorium. That answer is the life-nerve of the theater."[14]

II   Judith (1940)

The biblical figure of Judith, who in order to save her beseiged town of Bethulia makes her way into the enemy's camp, seduces their commander Holofernes, and then cold-bloodedly cuts off the aggressor's head while he sleeps beside her, would at first glance seem to provide an ideal mythic paradigm of the preventive action against tyranny which Anna Sophie Hedvig is meant to exemplify in modern terms. Yet, paradoxically enough, Abell's Judith explores the very obverse of this theme, the paralysis of action which is caused by doubt and vacillation. This curious and rather contrived inversion of the Judith legend and its dramatic traditions opened at the Royal Theater on February 10, 1940, barely two months before the German invasion of Denmark. Despite some interesting moments, the play was a failure—yet the causes of its ineffectiveness on the stage are in themselves so illuminating that they invite further critical scrutiny.

A number of playwrights before Abell—most notably Hebbel and Giraudoux—have been drawn to the Judith story and its powerful dramatic action. Friedrich Hebbel's early drama *Judith* (1840) concerns itself not with the apocryphal Jewish patriot and national heroine, but with the emotions of the woman behind the deed. Hebbel's focus on the complex weave of psychological, social, and sexual factors underlying Judith's relationship with Holofernes makes his play a fascinating precursor of modernism. Almost a century later, Jean Giraudoux's three-act tragedy *Judith* (1931) depicted a thoroughly modernized heroine, a witty and attractive young woman who flirts with the Bethulian officers, declines her grim mission at first, and who, when finally faced with the surprise of a thoroughly charming and gallant Holofernes, falls in love with her intended victim. Hebbel's Judith, though she too succumbs to the tyrant's charms, slays Holofernes out of pride. Giraudoux's intensely gallic heroine dispatches her Holofernes out of love. In both cases, however, the dramatic power of this character lies in her inevitable choice. Tragedy, Hebbel argues in *Mein Wort über das Drama* ("My Word about the Drama") (1843), arises from the operation of the will—"the obstinate extension of the ego"—and this phrase is an apt descriptor of the Judith archetype. Regardless of the motives which may be invented for her, Judith's character is inseparable from her action. Her deed becomes, as it were, the sole verification of her existence. Seen in this light, the totally unexpected, last minute reversal in Abell's interpretation—in which Judith does *not* slay Holofernes after all—vitiates the dramatic effect of the play. The result in performance was, Schyberg asserts, not merely undramatic but antidramatic. "It frustrates the audience's basic expectation, and the playwright thereby transgresses a fundamental rule of drama," this critic insists. "The suspense is not released, it simply disappears."[15]

Giraudoux's *Judith* (also that dramatist's least successful work) was Abell's acknowledged model; he had, we know, even watched Louis Jouvet rehearse the play at the Théâtre Pigalle during his stay in Paris. Whatever similarities may exist between the two works, however, are overshadowed by more important differences. Abell's heroine is in effect a double character, a less than convincing amalgamation of the ancient Judith and a modern society widow ("the

Widow in the Mirror in full-length portrait," Schyberg observed)
having no special knowledge of her biblical namesake ("Oh, that
Judith—the one in the Bible—actually I hardly know what it was
she did—or why. Yes, that's right, she went around with a severed
head in her beach towel"[16]). Once again in this play, Abell resorts to
an elaborate framework of high comedy within which to unfold his
fable. Stranded in a torrential downpour in the company of a nameless young man who has given her a lift, Judith seeks shelter in an
isolated country vicarage, where she is mistaken for a bride on her
honeymoon by the credulous old Fru Mynthe and soon finds herself
sharing the same guest room with the stranger. The promising im-
broglios and humorous repartee of this bizarre situation comedy—
rendered doubly entertaining in the hands of two such accomplished performers as Else Skouboe and Mogens Wieth—do
little, however, to prepare an audience for what is to follow. "All this
is witty, as [Gustav] Esmann was, and very charming, as Abell is,"
Svend Borberg declared in his review. "But it occupies nearly one-
third of the evening, and bears no relation whatever to Judith."[17]
Only when the young woman at last mentions her name, thereby
causing her companion to remember a biblical picture from his
childhood, does the main line of action begin to emerge:

YOUNG MAN.   Judith—it's you that that picture shows. Not Holofernes,
   he's only a minor character.
JUDITH.   Being called Judith is still not the same thing as being Judith.
YOUNG MAN.   Every woman is Judith—ought to be capable of acting as
   Judith did. How would you act?
JUDITH.   (laughing) I really have no idea—
YOUNG MAN.   It's so difficult to explain—I could spend all night telling
   about it.
JUDITH.   Then do—it's a long time until six or six-thirty.

                                                                      (39)

In a manner which tempts one to recall the fairy-tale comedies of
H. C. Andersen and his contemporaries, the young man's waking
dream of a biblical Judith "who concerns us all" magically
materializes. The vicarage's "little world of brightly flowered
wallpaper" fills with the sounds and sights of ancient Bethulia. The
sophisticated young widow finds herself plunged unwillingly into
the role of her mythic namesake—or, to be more accurate, the
mythic Judith is reduced by the playwright to the stature of her

weak-willed modern counterpart. The Giraudoucian costume drama into which Abell's play is thus transformed depicts a Bethulia at the mercy of the enemy's subtle war of nerves—a psychological war not unlike that which preceded Denmark's occupation.[18] "Every day at a particular time they fire off a rain of stones and arrows," the young man tells Judith, and yet

no one is hit, no one is killed. That's the finesse. It's this bloodless war that in the end will make their heads explode. Every day at the same time—after the last of the bells has fallen silent—the assault on their nerves begins. No one dares to breathe. Will what we're waiting for happen—will it happen today—? No, again it subsides—everyone slowly goes his way. Another new day of living has been granted—but it seems so precious that one dares hardly to use it. . . . (40)

Judith is chosen by the council of elders (prompted, perhaps, by the machinations of her ferociously unpleasant mother) to save her city from its misery by gaining access to Holofernes. Enclosed in her own barren preoccupation with the memory of a dead husband, however, she is indifferent to her responsibility. Only her paralyzed brother Dan (an image of Denmark?), the burning young zealot with crippled legs who symbolizes the will to action that lacks the means of accomplishing its goal, is capable of forcing her to recognize her duty. Abell, speaking through Dan, denounces "the well-dressed daughter from a rich house in a rich street" as

the high priestess of washed hands. The weak choose between oppression and clean hands—fear of getting themselves soiled keeps them down. While others go out and dig a barricade of earth against the sea, you sit at home and care for your hands. Nothing can arouse you before the water has covered the fields and reached your doorstep. Then you lift them up in lamentation towards heaven. But it is too late. (58)

The passionate confrontation between this figure, the play's most intensely conceived and disturbing character, and his sister is a dramatic highpoint that forcefully illustrates the thematic bifurcation of will and action, the gap "between the idea and the reality, between the emotion and the response" that concerns Abell as deeply as it did T. S. Eliot:

DAN.   (*after a pause*) If there is a God—(*after a pause*) you wanted him to speak to you—here. He has spoken—

JUDITH.   I will not go.
DAN.   You'll go.
JUDITH.   No one can force me.
DAN.   I can.
JUDITH.   You have no power over me any longer.
DAN.   In two hours the gates will be closed. Just before, you will leave
    home. The housemaids will follow you. You will make yourself beautiful.
    You are beautiful—so lovely that if I were . . . . You will use all your
    beauty aids—your hair must be fragrant—the fragrance must hide in the
    folds of your dress—and your eyes must be wide and shining—
JUDITH.   No!—no—(laughs) you imagine you can make me do it. But you
    have no power over me—not any longer. Your will is no longer mine. It
    was once—when we were children . . . everything you couldn't see from
    your little chair in the doorway you experienced through me. I was a
    voyager of discovery you sent forth. I perceived, you understood. Your
    will directed us both, just as though we were siamese twins. But we were
    separated. The last bonds with blood in them were severed by your
    words. We shall never again belong together.
DAN.   More than ever before.
JUDITH.   No!!
DAN.   Yes, I say! Like thought and action. I will go—and your feet will
    become mine. We are one—!
JUDITH.   No—
DAN.   We are two half corpses—who together will become one living
    being. I have my dead legs—you your dead husband.

                                                                    (55–56)

Moments later, as he presses the dagger into his sister's hand, Dan
reminds Judith that "the weak think their actions, the others per-
form them."

Thus literally mesmerized by Dan's hypnotic determination,
Abell's reluctant avenger, with fear "standing like a halo around her
head," sets out toward Holofernes' camp. In an expressionistic
scene entitled "In the Night Fog," fears and doubts pursue Judith
through layers of gauze, until she comes upon the play's other figure
of strength, the fiery Madam Branza. "The procuress, the brothel
madam, the slave trader, the city's most despised woman—that's
me," cries the sharp-tongued Branza, who has nothing but contempt for Judith's bourgeois values:

all those young friends of yours that you've ridden and danced and walked
with—they come down to me and my girls to seek comfort after you've
suddenly quit in the middle of the game and become the sensitive lily
because you're afraid to go further, or would rather wait for a higher bid.

Brothels shoot up like mushrooms after the night rain around women of your kind. . . . You're in exactly the same business as my girls, the only difference being that you only have one customer. . . .(69–70)

Branza's colorfully outspoken ill will is given a somewhat melodramatic explanation—the aging procuress cherishes an unrequited tenderness for Dan, one of her best customers, and she is therefore jealous of his more-than-fraternal longings for Judith—but these promising erotic entanglements are given no further attention by the playwright. Instead, Branza's wrath and Judith's anxiety inexplicably evaporate and, after joining hands in a kind of mutual communion with Dan's rebellious spirit, the two women set off bravely together to wreak vengeance on the enemy.

In the crucial scene in Holofernes' tent, the moment of crisis toward which the play and its subject must inevitably draw us, whatever dramatic tension has been generated in the Judith-Dan and Judith-Branza scenes is totally dissipated. Not only does Judith not slay Holofernes in Abell's version—she does not even succeed in exchanging a word with him. Disguised as a servant, he is hardly seen and remains silent throughout (a provocative bit of casting gave the part to an opera singer in the original production!). Instead of an adversary, the amiable young man from the rainstorm, now a counterfeit Holofernes planted by that wily tyrant to ensnare and kill the intruder "in self-defense," provides Judith with a convenient sounding board for her anguished philosophical ruminations about the relationship of faith and doubt, the responsibility of women to transform male tyranny, and the meaninglessness of things in general. Unaccountably, Holofernes permits the young couple, who become lovers in the course of their long, disquisitory night together, a full six hours for their deliberations! By sunrise, when Judith awakens to discover the implacable "servant" standing silently by her bedside, she has reached the fundamental realization that the tyrant is in fact no more than "the monument of our own weakness, of our fear of facing up to things"—"*we* are the soil in which he thrives," she says earlier (98)—and she decides that he

will not be slain by my hands—they are unworthy—
MADAM BRANZA. *(standing just behind the servant)* but by mine– *(The servant turns quickly; she stabs him with a dagger)* for they are the people's!
(The servant falls.)

(105)

Anyone remembering the class-conscious workman in *The Melody that Got Lost* and the similarly vigorous painter who descends to untangle the complications in *Eve Serves Her Childhood* will recognize in Madam Branza—symbol of the soundness and vitality of the common people—a favorite Abell device. Unfortunately, the point of her very abrupt, last-moment intervention was further obscured in production when a cautious censor deleted the last five words of her above speech! Nevertheless, despite objections by some reviewers that *Judith* seemed unclear or even "incomprehensible," lack of clarity is not this play's principal problem. An indictment of the apathetic, self-destructive tolerance of tyranny that thus reduces Holofernes himself to a mere supernumerary in Judith's drama does not unduly tax our powers of comprehension. Schyberg's additional observation that this diminution may also be seen as a reaction and protest against Kaj Munk's style of historical drama—in which, had Munk dramatized the story, Holofernes would almost surely have assumed titanic proportions—further illuminates the play's artistic logic. As comprehensible as this logic is, however, its premises remain to a significant extent antidramatic. The potential strength of will with which the mythic characters of Judith and Holofernes are so richly endowed is voided in order to make a philosophical point, and the dramatic clash of wills virtually inherent in this material is thereby sacrificed. "Of the biblical Judith, who in deep faith conceives the horrible plan herself, reveals it to no one, and carries it out with feminine cunning and dissimulation but also with the courage of an immense personality, there remains a rather thoughtless young lady who neither gets the idea nor acts on it," Borberg remarked in *Berlingske Tidende*. The same propensity for dealing in "words about action" rather than "words and action" which critics had recognized in *Anna Sophie Hedvig* also besets this play, but the "charming and amiable and confused young woman who listlessly allows herself to be driven halfway toward a goal, but who accomplishes nothing beyond falling in love with a lieutenant" was unable to provide the same unifying focus of interest that the character of Anna Sophie Hedvig represents on the stage.

A related problem undermining the effectiveness of *Judith* in performance is its lack of structural coherence. The pleasant but irrelevant comedy of the vicarage scenes and the casually introduced but undeveloped emotional relationships of the biblical portion of the drama obfuscate the main line of the action. Crucial scenes such as those in which Madam Branza first recognizes Holofernes and later stabs him are barely dramatized. At the close, the spurious "happy ending" that restores the amiable young lovers to a brave new world of Sunday morning sunshine and freshly baked bread is only superficially related to the dramatic issues with which the playwright has ostensibly been grappling.

There is no doubt that Abell himself was, as Elias Bredsdorff points out, deeply engaged in the larger ethical questions around which *Judith* revolves—"the conflict between weakness and strength, thought and action, doubt and faith."[19] The play remains among his most ambitiously "philosophical" works. Basically, however, Abell was neither a skilful debater like Shaw nor a brilliant dialectician like Sartre, and abstract ideas and verbose arguments are generally his worst enemies as a playwright. "He was," writes one critic bluntly but with considerable insight, "a great poet of the theater but an inferior thinker. He was a visionary, not an intellectual. And as a poet he lacked the ability or the will to give his thoughts clear, *unequivocal* expression." His dramatic powers failed him when (as in *Judith*) he "allowed ideas to proliferate at the expense of spontaneous theatrical creativity."[20] Much more often, though, his provocative and poetic style of theater represents a more controlled balance between idea and dramatic expression, a balance peculiarly illustrative of Hebbel's famous remark that "ideas are to the drama what counterpoint is to music: nothing in themselves but the *sine qua non* for everything."

III   *Five Years: 1940–1945*

"The soul of the theater is the living word," Abell wrote in his *Theater Sketches in Easter Weather*, first published in 1948. "Neither France's *roi soleil* nor England's virgin queen were able to subdue the freedom of the word, incessantly it changed disguises, costumes, bowed in apparent obsequiousness to the ruling royal box, attacked, smoothed over, attacked again, played hide-and-seek, rewrote itself, but was always itself—has always remained itself."[21] During the five years that German troops remained on Danish soil, Abell's embattled word-theater was obliged by necessity to adopt a more indirect, less outspoken tone, but his denunciations of moral passivity and political neutrality were never entirely silenced. "He always meant something different from what he said—it was like guessing a riddle," says one character about

another in *Dronning gaar igen* (*The Queen on Tour*),[22] Abell's only
serious play from these years—but the remark may also be taken as
a thinly disguised reminder of the playwright's own technique for
circumventing wartime censorship. As might be expected, the Nazi
occupation severely curtailed his major work as a dramatist. Instead,
as we have seen, he turned to other forms—ballet, satirical revues,
and film— for expression. Two Abell films from this period, "Tak
fordi du kom, Nick" ("Thanks for Coming, Nick", 1941) and "Reg-
nen holdt op" ("The Rain Stopped," 1942), have been extolled by
one critic as "perhaps the best comedies of Danish making seen on
the screen."[23] Incorporating themes and motifs familiar from his
plays, they offer more than a hint of Abell's largely unexploited
abilities as a screenwriter. *The Queen on Tour* was also at first
conceived as a film, but it was never produced and the script was
reworked by the author as a play, scrupulously "naturalistic" in its
believable use of time and place yet unmistakably symbolic in its
ringing defense of the free theater in which Abell always believed.

This three-act drama, the only Abell work seen on the legitimate
stage during the occupation years, was first acted at the Royal Theater on March 5, 1943—less than six months before the playwright
himself was arrested and imprisoned by the Gestapo. The original
version of the play, extant as a promptbook in the Royal Theater
library, was in general poorly received by the critics and was never
published. After the war, Abell attempted to revise and improve the
play for a production at Norway's Nationaltheatret in 1949, and this
text ultimately found its way into print, first in English translation
six years later. The revision was not performed in the dramatist's
own country until the acting company at Odense Theater undertook
to revive it for three special performances during the 1958–1959
season.

Although its theatrical impact has remained limited, *The Queen
on Tour* is remembered largely for its formidable central character,
an aging but indomitable actress called Mirena Pritz who "particularly at this time" feels compelled, in the face of all difficulties, to
tour the Danish provinces with her production of Shakespeare's
Hamlet, in which she plays Gertrude. It has become a "compulsive
necessity" for her to enact the story of the dreamer who "lives in the
midst of an Elsinore that has been made hostile and strange to him"
but who suddenly one day "smashes through the dissimulation to
become a man of realities, who dies for a purpose which is shared by

others." Mirena personifies Abell's vision of the theater as "more than mere canvas and plywood" but as "a part of life itself," and it is to this extraordinary prima donna that he gives the soaring declamatory tirades which constitute the play's thematic *raison d'être:*

I saw a world which would not be explained away—a world ruled by the brutal successors of Macbeth and Claudius, a world enclosed within a merciless Elsinore, with the ghosts of the past stalking the ramparts, and the future resting in the hands of the waverers—and up from that Elsinore towered my own fortress—not in defense, but as an attacking base. . . . Under the adopted names of the great and famous, I rode even into the most wretched of provincial towns, with a dagger concealed in every word—and in the audience there was always a Hamlet—a Hamlet, withdrawn into himself, clad in an armour of belief that one person—one person alone can achieve nothing. But is this Hamlet alone? No, Claudius is the solitary one—solitary in his hatred—the lord of hatred. Hatred, why do you not arise? Your flame could light armies of torches, and light up the heavens—and in that light we shall meet, and lay the ghosts in their graves—and together build a future! (169–70)

Even this relatively brief taste of Mirena's prolix, hortatory rhetoric makes it rather obvious that an actress of consummate ability and authority is wanted if this character is to become credible on the stage. In the Royal Theater the part was entrusted to Bodil Ipsen, perhaps the finest Danish actress to appear in this century, and the entire performance was centered around her remarkable, majestic personality. "Without Fru Ipsen, there would have been no play. It could not have been acted," declared Hans Brix in an otherwise rather self-indulgently sarcastic appraisal. "No one else could have carried through the long-winded title role with even a reasonable degree of success. And no playwright would dare to play this card without holding the queen in his hand."[24]

Mirena's denunciations of the spirit of compromise and her outspoken rhetorical tributes to freedom—"I wouldn't live without my freedom—freedom has always represented for me the most noble thing which mankind demands from life" (167)—carry topical political overtones which seem, under the circumstances, astonishingly bold. Through this character, Abell seeks to transpose the psychological and moral conflict faced by Shakespeare's Gertrude, who is torn between the demands of Claudius and Hamlet, to a political level, that is, to a dimension wherein Claudius is seen as the representative of the masculine world ruled by the destructive forces of brutality, egotism, and death. However, this theme, so important in Abell's later plays, is treated here only in adumbrated and ambiguous fashion. In general, the political sentiments animating Mirena's character and intended to arouse "the disheartened Hamlets in the auditorium" had, despite the force of Bodil Ipsen's acting and the explosive potential of the actual situation, only limited impact on contemporary theater audiences. The principal source of the play's weakness lay, in the view of many of its reviewers, in its elusive and misleading plot.

On the surface *The Queen on Tour* is a mystery *bouffe*. Ostensibly, both the ultrarealistic setting—the rustic public room of the provincial Sandskov Inn, an effective "synthesis of vulgarity and perfection" in Helge Refn's design—and the unusual but probable events which take place there late one evening place it squarely within an atmosphere of concrete reality uncommon in Abell's dramaturgy. The rollicking farce of a drunken country wedding party, complete with a soused groom afraid to go home with his weeping and manifestly pregnant bride, is counterpoised with the mysterious news of a dead man found on the Sørup road and a "ghostly apparition" covered with gold and pearls which has been seen in the same vicinity. The effectively prepared entrance of Mirena Pritz, still resplendent in the voluminous gilded costume she has worn for a miscarried *Hamlet* performance in a nearby hall and brandishing a revolver in order to gain a hearing and a meal, is a theatrical *coup* of the very broadest proportions. The gullible and frightened rustics lose no time in linking this astonishing creature with the murder of the dead man—particularly after the victim turns out to be the actress's box-office manager and supposed husband, Ivan Clehr ("Clehr isn't his real name—but I must say Hansen didn't suit him at all—he was—had been—a very refined man—you could see that just from the way he held his hands" (144)).

The unorthodox investigation carried on by a young county constable determined to expose Mirena's suspected complicity in the slaying reaches its culmination in her gargantuan "general confession"—an immense virtuoso monologue in which she admits not to murder, but to her "crime against those to whom I promised a supper, which they didn't get after all." The impulsive Mirena has, in short, interrupted the evening's performance in the sordid and depressing local theater to heap coals on the heads of the small handful of dull, petty, and inattentive spectators:

And I spoke my mind about those obtuse creatures, who imagine they are the guardians of culture, and never once realize that that which they call culture is a monstrously distorted caricature of something that ought to have been humanity's crowning glory! Their bodies, that were born that life might stream—yes, stream through them, had been changed, by themselves, into shells, which could only be given life by joiners and curtain-hangers, so as to make them move! But then not freely and unfettered—they could only move over doorsteps—from one vague sort of room to another—equally vague—sort of room. . . . I lashed the still waters until they foamed up in torrents! Like the well at Bethesda, when the angel descended to earth! Compromise! That was all their life! That was what these so-called cultured people existed on! Incomparable compromise, the marvellous virtue of which is that it is never compromising! That is the intellectual game, whereby people may be dead, whilst they are still alive! And they dare to call that culture! What terrible dread of culture! What terrible dread of truth and true culture! (141)

"An autobiography and an aesthetic essay on the actor's art," the effect of Mirena's soliloquy was, in Svend Borberg's estimation, "extraordinarily brilliant, but as a narrative and not as drama, and only Bodil Ipsen's fascinating personality could give the audience the illusion that this was theater."[25] Following the crucial events which this speech so graphically describes, and which cost the rest of the actors in the curtailed performance their supper money, Mirena has petulantly leaped from their touring bus and has made her way across the darkened countryside in full costume—to the consternation of the local inhabitants she encounters! She is joined at Sandskov Inn by Hamlet, Horatio, Laertes, and other fully costumed members of the *Hamlet* cast who have come in search of her, but only the vindictive Miss Lival—the company's Ophelia—bears her ill-will. She bitterly refutes Mirena's description of the useless and alcoholic Ivan Clehr ("half-dead upholstery and half played-out man") by insisting that the actress had in fact "succeeded in changing this handsome, elegant person, who was lacking in virility yet had the appearance of a man, into a poor drunken nitwit through her own terrific determination" (151). Her vicious allegation that the actress may in fact have killed Clehr in order to gain possession of an

inheritance which had recently come to him creates a suspenseful
second-act curtain. However, although obviously central to the dis-
pute, the shadowy character of Clehr himself—like that of Mrs.
Miller and Holofernes—remains a frustratingly abstract symbol left,
as Brix prefers to put it, "lying outside on the highway, a poor
carrion."

Nevertheless, although most of the principal action in the play has
been talked about rather than shown, Frederik Schyberg's long and
painstaking review is fair in remarking that, up to this point, "surprise follows on surprise, development on development, contrast on
contrast, and the audience is irresistibly drawn from the initially
adopted tone of merry and fantastic mystery comedy into the serious, more genuinely exciting drama."[26] Even this rather partial
critic is forced to concede, however, that the weak third act "rather
represents a falling curve and offers at any rate a resolution which is
unsatisfyingly confusing and disappointing to the audience." "Mists
of fog descended in front of any even halfway reasonable conclusion," Borberg added with less diplomacy. In the final act, a wholly
irrelevant romantic triangle involving the barmaid, a latecomer
called Gustav, and the wife with whom he is (inexplicably) reunited
is suddenly brought to the foreground—though heavy cuts in the
promptbook indicate that it was made less intrusive in the original
production. Meanwhile, the significant and visually effective thematic contrast which has been suggested between the mores of the
"real" world of Sandskov and the "art" of the costumed theater
people—"We are the dreams humanity has of cutting its way out
from everyday life! Is it, then, capable of judging us? Never!"
(145)—is abruptly sidetracked. The interest of the mystery plot is
also defused: Mirena confesses to having fired off two random shots
at the tires of the bus but, although one of them *may* accidently have
struck Clehr, the heavily intoxicated victim was in fact killed by an
unidentified hit-and-run driver. To further obscure matters by re-
moving the alleged inheritance motive, we learn that Clehr was
never Mirena's legal husband after all! If Abell thus aborts his play's
previous lines of development, he spreads additional confusion by
introducing new, unprepared themes. In the 1943 production version, Mirena came suddenly to assume an Anna Sophie Hedvig
posture, insisting on her inviolable right to slay her victim "in cold
blood like an animal" provided the proper ethical circumstances
were present—an unexpected development that, as the play's re-

viewers were quick to insist, made absolutely no sense in the light of the contradictory premise that the actress's revolver shots had been neither intentionally homicidal nor the real cause of death. This version's closing moments, in which the zealous young constable decides to drop his investigation and shouts up to Mirena's room that she is "free to go," merely exacerbated the already vague and nebulous impression left by the final act. In his published revision of *The Queen on Tour*, Abell tries to address these problems by providing his central character with a more decisive and affirmative response to the situation, but the result is not entirely successful. Although Clehr, as we have seen, is associated (in a very tenuous way, to be sure) with the "brutal successors of Macbeth and Claudius," Mirena admits to having killed him, by providential accident, "in the heat of the moment, out of petty hatred." When the constable assures her that the official cause of death is the motor vehicle accident, she replies ambiguously but with dignity: "I am my own judge" (171). As she is about to use the revolver on herself, Gustav comes forward to speak to her of his own "talent for living" and her part in it: "I saw your Hamlet—there in the audience there is always a Hamlet—you gave me a reason for my life." Appropriately recalled to her own true mission, she hands over the pistol, gathers her band of players about her once more, and drives off with them in triumph—at two o'clock in the morning! "I suppose everybody has his third act—the climax comes in the third act," says the great actress with more than a touch of the playwright's own wistful self-irony behind the words. "My third act was beyond my capabilities" (168).

Whatever dramaturgical flaws or concessions to the censor may have clouded Abell's meaning in *The Queen on Tour*, no one—least of all the German occupation force—could be in doubt about the strength of personal conviction and integrity that lay behind it. As the political situation worsened, further public expression of the playwright's views became impossible. On August 29, 1943, the German high command proclaimed Denmark to be in a "state of emergency"—a measure which thereby deposed the Danish civil government, instituted harsher curbs on personal freedom, and inaugurated a period of intensified resistance and sabotage. In the early morning hours, hundreds of hostages from Danish cultural life, including Abell himself, were rounded up by the Gestapo and imprisoned for a time in a concentration camp at Horserød. Abell's

release only served to sharpen his commitment to resist Nazi aggression. Like Nordahl Grieg, to whose memory he devoted an
illegally printed (and obviously anonymous) obituary in 1944, he
rejected the dangerously easy "humanism" which "feels a disgust at
injustice, but is unwilling to fight for what is just."[27] With great
personal courage, he responded impulsively to one of the occupation's darkest acts of terrorism, the brutal assassination by Gestapo
thugs of his brilliant "rival" in the Danish theatre, Kaj Munk. On
the evening of January 5, 1944, when the murder of the
playwright-priest the previous night had become known, Abell
rushed on to the stage of the Royal Theater, interrupting the performance in progress in order to pay tribute to his memory. Arrest
and severe punishment by the Gestapo would have been swift if
Abell had not definitively disappeared underground for the remainder of the war. During the last sixteen months of the occupation, his
famous elegance transformed by dyed hair and a moustache, the
playwright lived in intimate contact with the resistance movement;
the artistic fruit of this experience became *Silkeborg*, the most significant drama to emerge from the five war years.

IV   Silkeborg *(1946)*

In Denmark as elsewhere in the western theater world, the
events of World War II gave rise to a mixed aftermath of "war"
plays, including, among the most notable, Leck Fischer's *Fronten
(The Front)*, Soya's *Efter (After)*, and Munk's historical drama *Niels
Ebbesen*. Within this broad category, however, no play matched the
impact and ambitious scope of Kjeld Abell's *Silkeborg*, still regarded
by many critics as "the most important and dramatically successful
of the various Danish plays dealing with the period of German
occupation."[28] No simple Resistance panegyric, *Silkeborg* is a
searching examination of the shortsighted indifference and hypocrisy as well as the courage of the author's countrymen during these
years. The play's first production, staged less than ten months after
the Allied liberation of Denmark, spoke in bold and moving terms to
contemporary audiences. "This is what theater is for," declared
Frederik Schyberg in a persuasively balanced review in *Politiken*
(March 2, 1946). "The production has faults and flaws, but on the
whole it fulfills the true mission of theatrical art: to force us, as
audience, to think and to recognize."[29] Although many of the play's
first reviewers echoed Carsten Nielsen's indignant view that the

Royal Theater had "blemished its honor and its conscience by refusing (regardless of the form and the excuse)" Abell's new work,[30] its less perfectly polished production at the New Theater, directed by Sam Besekow and seen for no fewer than 107 consecutive performances, nevertheless left no doubt of its stageworthiness and emotional force. "In it," Schyberg's review concluded, "we can recognize ourselves, with anger, with regret, with pleasure, or with a shudder." Today, although this sense of the play's acute topical immediacy is obviously absent and its political simplifications and exhortations may appear at times less than convincing, a revival or rereading of *Silkeborg* still offers ample evidence of its dramatic effectiveness. In its own time, as one historian of the postwar period points out, it formed part of the crucial turning point that marked "the *artistic* liberation of the theater which had been underway throughout the thirties, and which was now to dominate the world's stages under the rubric, 'the poetic theater.' "[31]

Silkeborg also marks a turning point in its author's own artistic development. In its form this play, which functions both as a symbolic fantasy and, within its "poetic" framework, as a realistic drama of the wartime conflicts and complications which beset a typical provincial family, looks ahead toward the more complex symbolic dramas of Abell's later career. Although the structural device of a framing action is, as we have already seen, a favorite one even in Abell's early plays, in *Silkeborg* he provides a dreamplay framework which merges present and past in a much more unfettered concurrency, creating in the process "a timeless theater in which the living and the dead pass one another in the fashions and clothing of shifting generations."[32] The play's complicated "overture," which takes place on Himmelbjerget, the lovely scenic hilltop overlooking the Silkeborg lakes in central Jutland, takes the form of an impressionistic kaleidoscope of successive August 29s that lead, ultimately, to that dark date in 1943 when the Nazi overlords proclaimed their "state of emergency" in Denmark. The point of departure in Abell's imaginative voyage through time is August 29, 1905—a matchless summer day in whose magic, shimmering brightness "no one is dead. Everything lives and comes to life again. Past and future stand like mirages in the summer heat."[33] The character of the Student, caught in a kind of waking dream while his less receptive companion dozes, is carried forward through time, and experiences brief glimpses of his country's "future" history—World War I, the Armis-

tice heralded by a skeptical and unhappy Angel of Peace, the un-
heeded rise of Nazism in the thirties, and finally the occupation
itself. As swift glimpses are presented of these historical moments,
filtered through the consciousness of the Student, there also unfolds
the more commonplace domestic history of a middle-class Silkeborg
family, comfortably indifferent to the world around them. "I admit
I'm not really clear about the Jewish question," declares the smugly
"sober-minded" businessman Martinsen-Smith, lineal descendant
of the numerous paternal tyrants who inhabit Abell's earlier plays,
during one of the family's annual picnic-pilgrimages to Himmelbjerget on an August 29 in the mid-1930s: "But we certainly
must take care not to dismiss them out of hand. It wouldn't hurt us
to learn one or two things here at home. Just look at unemployment.
Simply abolished. By a dictate from above. Just like that. Not
bad—and surely worth taking a closer look at." (17) Twenty years
but only four pages earlier, at the start of World War I, this cautious
and morally myopic character was saying, with unconcealed admira-
tion, that "there's one thing you have to grant" his warlike neighbors
to the south. "They're clever, damned clever. They know what
precision and order mean. And without those two things, you won't
ever get anywhere" (13). Throughout the play's introductory historical montage, this irony of uncommented juxtaposition carries strong
weight.

    Determined to protect Git, the daughter who is born to the
Martinsen-Smiths at the beginning of the play, from her "monstrosity of a family," the Student names himself her self-appointed
"godfather"—thereby forging a bond between the imaginative universe of the framework and the realistic events which occupy the
main body of the drama. Brief snatches of Git's early life are perceived through the eyes of the Student on Himmelbjerget, and on
her thirty-eighth birthday—which occurs on August 29, 1943—his
annual greeting to his adopted spiritual godchild brings the overture
to a close. This letter's purpose is thematic, intended to articulate
the words of homage to the Danish resistance movement which lie
embedded in the playwright's evocative title:

Silkeborg. A silken castle *(borg)*. A fortified town with towers and peaks of
sheerest silk. For an enemy it must be difficult to attack. Everywhere he
meets only silk that waves and floats and yields. If he strikes, he strikes in a
pillow which makes no sound. . . . And just when everything seems to be

at its laziest and most supple, when everything droops most good-naturedly and submissively, the wind may suddenly turn, become like a hurricane, and make the pliant silk stand taut and resoundingly firm like a mighty banner that sweeps everything down. (22)

Although a later critic of *Silkeborg* has called this particular passage the play's "only formal blemish," dismissing it as "symbolism for fashion designers,"[34] such a view overlooks the fundamental emotional impact of the image at a given time and place, upon a theater audience that would be responsive to the full range of associations inherent in Abell's felicitous choice of Silkeborg—the idyllic country town near which Kaj Munk's brutally mistreated body was discovered, through whose streets the martyred priest's funeral procession passed, and which lived throughout the occupation in the shadow of the German headquarters in Silkeborg Sanatorium. Abell's deeply nationalistic play touches all of these chords.

Any sense of celebratory flag-waving is far outweighed, however, by the playwright's indictment of the narrow-mindedness and passivity that permit a Holofernes or a Hitler to flourish—an indictment which transcends the limits of the historical circumstances which inspired it. The family drama which is the real heart of the play observes a naturalistic compression of time and space that contrasts sharply with the open atmosphere of the Himmelbjerg fantasy which frames it. Within the walls of the bourgeois Martinsen-Smith household, in the space of less than twenty-four hours, Abell swiftly precipitates a crisis which brings each of his major characters to a decisive moment of choice or enlightenment. The realistic context for this drama is the winter of sabotage and violence which followed the explosive events of August 29. It had originally been the dramatist's intention to use Munk's funeral cortege in January 1944—the details of which he eagerly solicited from his comrades in the resistance movement—to incite his placid provincial family to action. In the play as we have it, this climactic moment has been translated into a more personal, intensely immediate dramatic situation.

The three generations represented in the Martinsen-Smith family album are as sharply divided as the oddly partitioned living room in which they gather during the opening family scenes—an interior which is physically separated into three visually incongruous areas but which "nevertheless appears to form a whole." The youngest

generation is represented by the eighteen-year-old grandson
Jørgen, already a resistance activist and editor of an illegal newspaper, who is preparing in the first scene to join a sabotage mission
to which his nervous, rather self-indulgent personality makes him
peculiarly ill suited. Outspokenly enraged by the complacency and
hypocrisy of his middle-class milieu, he is nonetheless shaped and
rendered vulnerable by it as well. Jørgen is a familiar Abell type, not
unlike the character of John in *Anna Sophie Hedvig*. His mother
Git, the play's focal figure, is another Widow in the Mirror, the
image of a refined but ineffectual humanism which dares not choose
or take the consequences of a choice.[35] After the death of her un-
mourned husband—a colorless young man who soon became for Git
"just a well-tailored suit and an impeccable hair parting" (54)—she
has been content to retreat into an oblivious shadow existence of
fastidious reluctance. "You're weak in a very charming and very
disastrous way," her plainer and more rebellious sister Thyra tells
her, while confessing that she has hated "the fools who were unable
to see how pale and blond and indifferent" Git really was (69). Thyra
herself (a role which afforded Beatrice Bonnesen a rewarding personal triumph in the original production) is Git's antithesis, the
disappointed and sharp-tongued spinster who has been cheated of
life, and who now seizes the chance to "fling herself into an almost
erotic relationship to the world situation" (40). In many ways a
darker and more dissonant variant of the frustrated Aunt Missia in
the comedy *Eve Serves Her Childhood.* The eldest of the three
generations, represented by Martinsen-Smith and his conventional
wife, embodies the accepted values and prejudices of the mercantile
middle class at which Abell has so often before taken aim.
Martinsen-Smith, a house tyrant who would readily endorse the
views of the Grandfather in *Eve* or the Father in *Anna Sophie
Hedvig*, congratulates himself on his "sober-mindedness" and takes
refuge, for as long as he is able, in his "efforts to view a thing from as
many sides as possible" (34). Given this brief roll call one might well
fear that, as Schyberg's review observed, Abell "would repeat himself by depicting his 'bourgeois family' yet one more time." However, this critic continues, "the events of the war years have given
him a new experience, and a wider and more biting causticity."

Whatever the reason for its presence, the tone of more robust and
stinging directness to which Schyberg refers does set *Silkeborg*
apart from the earlier plays. From the very outset, character con-

frontations partake of a new vehemence and straightforwardness. "It's as if you sometimes forget that we're at war," Thyra tells her father and the mendacious collaborators he has been entertaining at dinner:

MARTINSEN-SMITH. War—? Pish-pash and poppycock. What you people call war, who has brought it down on our heads? You—nobody else.

THYRA. Fortunately, emotions cannot always be suppressed.

MARTINSEN-SMITH. Emotions must be controlled. That is the badge of culture.

THYRA. Naturally! Control yourself to bits and pieces until you end up either in the madhouse, or else in a toothless neutrality that's unable to say yes or no—but just bow and scrape. But no matter how small you are, or how little space you take up on a map, if you can't answer with a clear yes or a clear no, you have no right to exist.

MARTINSEN-SMITH. And if so and so many human lives are wasted in the process, what do you care. But if you could only ask the dead—

THYRA. They are the most alive of all of us.

MARTINSEN-SMITH. You'll forgive me if I prefer not to become one of your dead?

THYRA. You never will.

MARTINSEN-SMITH. Couldn't a stray bullet strike me down tomorrow?

THYRA. Yes, a stray one.

MARTINSEN-SMITH. Gamblers have to take their chances—is that what you mean?

THYRA. I would never have put it like that.

MARTINSEN-SMITH. Ye gods! What sort of a world are we living in? . . .

(38)

Although *Silkeborg* operates with many of the same basic types that populate other war plays, notably Fischer's *The Front,* its characters spring to life through the complexity and even the ambiguity of their personal responses to the play's abstract ethical conflicts—neutrality vs. activism, the compromises of the old vs. the absolutes of the young, selfish individualism vs. shared responsibility. "The turbidity of our motives and the involved consequences of our actions, herein lies the tragedy, herein lies the pain," writes one critic.[36] Though the wrong-headed reviewer for *Berlingske Tidende* is right enough in stating that Abell "both reveals and conceals" the psychology of his characters and even in adding that his characters are frequently "filled with gauze-enveloped complexes" that complicate their motives, he is surely misled in his conclusion that a writer "cannot reveal any truth whatsoever through veiled characterizations."

The dramatic climax around which the play revolves is created through the presence of two thematically related characters from outside the Martinsen-Smith family circle. Both function as catalysts, and both end as victims of these weak and irresolute people. Carl Otto, the German-born cousin of Git and her childhood sweetheart in the fleeting Himmelbjerg summers of the past, has now returned to Silkeborg as a military officer in the occupation force; an unwilling captive of Hitler's war machine, he has realized too late the high price of passive acquiescence in tyranny. Carl Otto's hopeless love for Git brings on his own meaningless and tragic destruction at the hands of the jealous and self-willed Jørgen. Git's emotionally undependable son is also responsible, albeit indirectly, for the death of Little Ulriksen, his comrade in the resistance movement and the play's most positive character, at the hands of the Nazis. Ulriksen, the robust young man of the people who, like Madam Branza in *Judith*, is neither impaired by his milieu nor hampered by private emotions, embodies the playwright's tribute to the Danish resistance and his faith in the reliability of common humanity. In a very important sense, meanwhile, Little Ulriksen, the resistance fighter, is allied by Abell with the enemy soldier Carl Otto. "In these two figures," observes Svend Erichsen, "he pays homage to the energy of the human spirit, the antithesis of passivity."[37] Though they never meet, they stand as mutually complementary forces, and with his shrewd sense for scenic effect Abell makes them the play's thematic spokesmen.

The emotional highpoint in *Silkeborg* remains its fourth scene, depicting the frank, face-to-face confrontation between Carl Otto and Git. Although prompted by his personal feelings, so painfully bound up with memories of their botched relationship and the realization of his own disappointed existence since, Carl Otto's visit to the apprehensive, indecisive Git in her family's home is designed much more as a public than a private scene. Discussion rather than emotion provides the forward thrust. Carl Otto's unhappy personal history is seen only as "a lovely footnote" to the wider ideological and ethical concerns which underlie this episode and the play as a whole. "The playwright succeeds in making his German a human being," Schyberg declared, "not in order to defend him" but in order to deliver a harsh indictment of the moral complicity of Git and the society for which she stands.

Abell's illusionless raisonneur, a "thwarted suicide" for whom not even self-destruction has succeeded, recognizes all too clearly his own guilt, incurred as a silent and compliant witness to the horrific developments of the thirties in Germany. But "all that never even existed at that time," Git protests:

CARL OTTO.   Eight years ago—? It was in full bloom.
GIT.   No, not in the same way.
CARL OTTO.   Just the same as today.
GIT.   All that with the Jews perhaps. I'm ashamed of myself when I think back on how quickly one made do with the excuse that such a problem must surely be very different with you than with us. But that other business, who took that seriously? Those ridiculous caperers who heil'ed around in their unbecoming uniforms, you could only laugh at them.
CARL OTTO.   That is where you sealed our doom.

(55)

"We who could neither see nor hear, we should have been sentenced to death," he adds a few moments later. "Instead it became life imprisonment for all." Widening his harsh indictment, however, Carl Otto also rips through Git's own self-satisfaction and complacency in order to lay bare what for Abell's audience was a still more distasteful truth:

You imagine yourselves to be sitting in the midst of the most shining innocence. Only after a certain date were you dragged into the picture. But what about before—? Where were you all before—? Weren't you just exactly as blind as we were—? What did your newspapers, your ministers, your public opinion say—? You were still living in a democracy with freedom of religion, freedom of speech, and all sorts of other freedoms. What did you use them for—? (57)

The questions multiply, and they admit of no easy answers. Although he readily acknowledges the courage of the young men who, as Git phrases it, "tower above your wretchedness" and have "become our backbone," Carl Otto, speaking for Abell, has this warning: "One day they may suddenly turn against you, and call you to judgment. They are fighting for you. But did you fight for them?"

(58) In this scene, the war "intrudes upon the Martinsen-Smith family and exposes them," as Schyberg remarked in his review. "They are at the same time the victims and the guilty. They are struck hard—but they are struck in particular because they are inadequate human beings."

Their antithesis is Little Ulriksen, who is depicted with none of the traits of their middle-class mentality, and whose untragic figure is viewed—not without sentimentality—as the embodiment of the young men "who gave their lives so that we could live on without having to be ashamed and cast down our eyes every time we look at ourselves in a mirror" (79). On the night of Carl Otto's visit to Git, Ulriksen has taken Jørgen on his first active resistance mission. The type of RAF weapon drop in which they participate (an operation which, we are told, the playwright insisted upon experiencing at first hand) is described by Ulriksen earlier in the play with such verbal evocativeness that the subsequent staging of the actual episode seems superfluous. For all his matter-of-factness, Little Ulriksen is prone to sheer romantic eloquence at the thought of Agnes, code name for the "angel with arms filled with lovely weapons" whose arrival they anxiously await:

It's enough to give you a damn lump in the throat. Except that you don't have time. You take your bicycle. Way the hell out in the country. Everything has to go like clockwork. But still your inner thoughts, they're not here. They're over there. On a pitch-dark windy airfield in Scotland or somewhere in those parts. The grass lies flat in the storm from the propellers. Slowly and unsteadily they turn in onto the runway. Up into the wind—! There—! Now they dash along the cement like huge sandpipers on a beach. Umph—! With a load like that you can barely get off the ground. But they do—! And then they're up there in the night. On their way to a microscopic spot on the map where we stand and wait. It's one goddamn beautiful piece of work. (29)

The speech itself, at least in the original, offers a revealing example of Abell's inevitable tendency to permit all his characters, regardless of psychological or social differences, to speak in the same articulate but sometimes dramatically improbable tone of voice—that of the playwright himself.

When the weapon drop described by Ulriksen miscarries, the two young conspirators flee to Jørgen's house, where the latter's thoughtless outbursts of jealousy and petulance upon discovering traces of his mother's male visitor cost them their escape. As the Germans storm the house, Little Ulriksen, after having first ensured Jørgen's safety, dies in a hail of bullets. However, the dead are seen here as "the most alive of all of us"—and the sense of Little Ulriksen's presence is intended to permeate the tense scene of partial resolution which follows his death. Martinsen-Smith, who has been taken into custody by the Germans during the raid and has been released on the condition that he turn in his grandson in return, is brought to recognize at least something of his past misguidedness:

> I understand nothing. All my life I have lived in a world that made decisions beforehand on my behalf. My imagination can't take it in. It has shrunk to an old dry walnut that rattles around inside my head. . . . You mustn't expect that I should be able to understand.
> GIT. Father. I didn't understand either. Not until last night. A friend, a childhood companion I hadn't seen in years, explained the beginning. Little Ulriksen showed me the rest.
>
> (78)

Moments later, the approaching sounds of Little Ulriksen's funeral procession, calling to mind Kaj Munk's cortege, draws the family drama to its climax. However, only Jørgen and the audience are able to hear the steps of the dead passing outside, this "army of nameless ones who have never wanted a name." Significantly, the rest of the family can hear nothing—and Jørgen's angry eulogy over his friend questions their real willingness to abandon their own selfish interests for the common good, the only means of attaining true freedom. "I know you. I know you from myself, from everything that you've heaped up around me and inside of me—and I don't trust you an inch," he tells them (80). Yet almost at once, this unreliable individualist compromises his loudly professed collectivist ideals when he shoots the hapless and unsuspecting Carl Otto in a rage of purely personal frustration and jealousy. On this dissonant and rather melodramatic note, the play proper closes.

The endeavor in the final scene to resolve this note into a triumphant fanfare seems, when stripped of the context in which *Silkeborg* was originally performed, less than wholly convincing. This epilogue—a conciliatory coda which attempts to restore the mood of fantasy and vision established in the overture—takes place on the play's final August 29, in the unquiet summer of 1944. The turn-of-the-century Student is about to awaken from his extraordinary "dream" of the future ("Have nearly forty years gone by—or has everything you have perceived been perceived in one single glimpse?"), and the Angel of Peace and Little Ulriksen join forces to urge him (and the audience) to recognize the moral of his vision: "You hoped and believed that the idea of humanity could be defended with intellectual weapons, but . . . it cannot be done by cultivating your own little garden and your own clear conscience. The goal must be a common conscience—and that is achieved only through struggle." (82) Inspired by the dead resistance fighter to a new awareness of his future "mission" in society, the Student sets off toward Silkeborg "to fight."

Shrouded in the proliferation of these rather abstract ideas, the contours of the realistic character relationships with which we have been chiefly concerned throughout the play lose their sharpness. The reconciled sisters Git and Thyra try, though without much conviction, to reassure the guilt-ridden Jørgen that his deliberate killing of Carl Otto was no more than "the slaying of a uniform." Meanwhile, Martinsen-Smith and his generation, whose mendacity and passivity have rendered them responsible for the scourge of Nazism (at least in terms of the play's logic), are left out of the final picture entirely. "The fact is," Hans Brix was moved to observe in his review, "that the play, rather than being about human destinies, is about opinions, ideas, above all one idea, Kjeld Abell's view of our current problem. This view assumes that active communism, ruthless action, is the road forward toward humanity for all."[38]

Valid only up to a point, however, Brix's criticism oversimplifies the play's ethical stance, reducing an essentially emotional and lyrical spirit of revolt in Abell's writing to an inadequate political label. Perhaps a more illuminating analogue to Abell's rejection of passivity and easy pessimism in these circumstances is Archibald Mac-Leish's somewhat earlier repudiation of those "irresponsibles" who, given the weapon of words, refused to take the weapon and "carry it to the barricades of intellectual warfare, to the storming of belief, the fortifying of conviction where alone this fighting can be won."[39] Later, Abell's prominent contemporary H. C. Branner was to write: "It is no use that an artist says to himself that one is unable, alone out of everyone, to give mankind back its lost faith in life, that one is unable, with his limited understanding, to think the new thoughts and form the new images which will teach the world to live without war. Because there is no one else able to do it. And one does what it is necessary to do."[40] It is in this wider sense that Abell's playwriting constitutes engaged, deliberately provocative, and hence "political" theater.

For all this, however, *Silkeborg*—to the extent that it does succeed in doing so—holds our attention as a drama, rather than as a political or ideological tract. Its indictment of passivity and compromise is forceful because it expresses itself in terms of meaningful character conflicts. As such, it reaches beyond the limits of a particular set of historical circumstances. The play's ability to draw its characters into what Kenneth Tynan calls "a desperate situation" as well as its deft amalgamation of realism and fantasy represent noteworthy developments in its author's technique.

Both in terms of style and subject matter, *Silkeborg* is closely related to the three other Abell plays from this period which, for the sake of convenience, have been considered together as "political drama." Each explores, as it were, a particular facet of the basic Sartrean conflict between selfish passivity and free and responsible commitment to a moral choice. All four works address themselves, with varying directness, to the rise of fascist tyranny, and in each of them the taking of a human life becomes the litmus test for its philosophical argument. Anna Sophie Hedvig's unexpected positive action is counterbalanced by the biblical Judith's equally unexpected inaction. Mirena Pritz, like Hugo in Sartre's *Dirty Hands,* is obliged to find the right reason for an ambiguous act, and the turbid motivation for her deed complicates the issue still further. Finally, the group drama of the Martinsen-Smith family tries to confront a situation of wartime conflict fraught with still greater ambivalence and complexity. Unlike most conventional war plays, it offers little sense of victorious celebration. Its concluding triumphant fanfare seems largely spurious, for one is left with a feeling of inconclusiveness and of a struggle that lies ahead.

CHAPTER 4

Fantasias

I Days on a Cloud (1947)

SURVEYS of Kjeld Abell's work often group the three-act drama *Dage på en Sky (Days on a Cloud)*, which had its premiere at the Royal Theater on December 11, 1947, among his so-called "political" plays. Its background, we are reminded, was the atomic bombing of Hiroshima on August 6, 1945, and the postwar nuclear age of pessimism and fear which that event suddenly inaugurated. Although the play's first reviewers had generally lavish praise for Holger Gabrielsen's minutely coordinated and sensitively interpreted production, a storm of newspaper controversy—comparable in acerbity to the uproars that had greeted some of Ibsen's plays three-quarters of a century earlier—quickly erupted over its political implications. On the one hand, Abell was chastised for lack of clarity in this complex metaphysical fable ("like so many before him, he strands in the quicksand, quagmire, and abyss of abstractions," Brix declared[1]); on the other hand, he found himself the victim of a virtual witch-hunt, instigated by detractors who denounced the play for its alleged "antidemocratic" and "pro-Soviet" sentiments. Its author's response to these distortions had little effect: "They call *Days on a Cloud* unclear and incomprehensible, while at the same time they insist that it is about iron curtains. Isn't it incredible that something so obscure can yield something so clear? I know nothing about iron curtains!"[2] As misleading and irrelevant to the play's artistic intent as such a dogmatic political interpretation of it may seem to a reader today, there can be no doubt that this determined opposition to Abell, "couched as it was in the cold war's remorseless tone of either-or," had a lasting effect on his popularity and the direction of his subsequent development.[3] Moreover, with disappointing frequency, later commentators on the work, often satisfied to schematize its purported "ideology" or else to attach such evasive labels as "verbose" and "capricious," have failed to come to critical terms with one of the modern Scandinavian theater's richest and most challenging poetic achievements.[4]

Both in style and in theme, *Days on a Cloud* declares a noteworthy change in Abell's playwriting. It is the first of a series of what may be termed imaginative "fantasias," purposefully nonrepresentational and associational and centering on the theme of self-destruction as an act of escape and (negative) isolation from the human dilemma. The concomitant shift in environment and ambience is striking. From the recognizable precincts of Jacob Ærekærsvej, Thorvaldsen's Museum, Sandskov Inn, and Silkeborg, we are transported in these later works to the realm of dreams, to Iselø, Minikoi, Villa Mayerling, and to the desolate cloudscape in which this play takes place. Fantasy, however, is never for Abell a romantic flight from reality or a mere playground for "a self-indulgent machinery that want[s] only to be set in motion, turning, spinning, demonstrating its technical delights."[5] Throughout this new phase of his writing, his insistent belief in a provocative verbal theater, capable of confronting the spectator with dangerous truths, remains strong. "There must be something to conquer, not just something to entertain," the statue of Holberg tells the statue of Oehlenschläger in the little playlet entitled "Night on Kongens Nytorv." "The theater is a fairy-tale world at war with the world outside."[6] In *Days on a Cloud*, Aphrodite comes to realize that "from doubt to faith is only a hair's breadth"[7]—and Abell was convinced that the theater was peculiarly suited to closing that gap.

As an indictment of escapist humanism and intellectual apathy, Abell's new play restated an abiding concern of his foregoing "realistic" dramas. However, the scope of the play's symbolic philosophical conflict—between the passive, Olympian, death-bringing values of the male world of the gods and the actively engaged and responsible attitude of the female world of Aphrodite—is both more ambitious and more encompassing than in any of his previous works. The central dramatic situation around which this expressionistic fantasia revolves is, meanwhile, simple enough. The action takes place in the mind of the play's sole male character, a disillusioned scientist-physician called He, during the split seconds between his suicidal plunge from an aircraft and his existential decision to release his parachute instead. These fleeting seconds are expressed as days spent on a cloud in the heavenly regions through which he falls—a cloud populated by goddesses of Greek mythology who live a disconsolate existence among ruined temples and crumbling pillars. Caught up in the symbolic struggle between their realm, held together by the constructive forces of love, and the masculine world of Zeus and the gods, ruled by the negative forces of power, egotism, and death, "He" is eventually brought to recognize his own escapist self-betrayal and to reaffirm his responsibility to the former values. At the conclusion of the play, he reaches the decision to live.

Affinities with the dramatic vision of Jean-Paul Sartre, whose existential drama *The Flies* had been seen at the Royal Theater one year before Abell's play, are readily apparent in *Days on a Cloud*. The Sartrean theme of engaged commitment rings clearly in Aphrodite's statement: "The law says that he who steals the holy fire pays with his life. But the penalty should be heavier still if the fire dies in law-abiding hands. The choice is free" (81). In rejecting "a theater of characters" and character psychoanalysis in his seminal essay "Forgers of Myths" (1946), Sartre called instead for "a theater of situation" in which the protagonist "chooses, whether he wishes to or not, for everyone else when he chooses for himself."[8] In precisely this sense, the crucial choice by Abell's modern Icarus to rescind his fall and transform it instead from a negative to a positive act profoundly affects every other level of action in the drama. Sartre's objective is a theater which addresses the audience's "most general preoccupations, dispelling their anxieties in the form of myths which anyone can understand and feel deeply." To this very end, Abell has endeavored to forge a myth capable of projecting "an enlarged and enhanced image" of the fragmentation and anxiety of the nuclear age. (The extent to which his play does in fact project an image which, in Sartre's terms, "anyone can understand and feel deeply" must, of course, be said to be a bone of some contention!) The first reviewers of Abell's unusual experiment expressed their discomfort at the apparent disregard of conventional character analysis and clarity of "motivation": "the realistic backgrounds of the characters themselves are kept in a half-light which, if it is intentional, cannot avoid causing irritation," even Schyberg declared. "Why must we *guess* so much?"[9] However, Sartre might well have reminded them, as he did the unreceptive New York reviewers of the Broadway rendering of Anouilh's *Antigone*, that they were again applying critical assumptions derived from a "theater of characters" to a theater phenomenon of a different order entirely.

Poised within the controlling perspective of the central figure's deflected suicide, a number of intersecting planes of action contribute to the play's complex dramatic rhythm. Closely intertwined and only gradually developed in the course of the drama, these areas of conflict and tension may be examined separately. The most encompassing of them is the symbolic struggle that is waged between the male world of Zeus and his cronies and the female world of the goddesses who intercept the falling parachutist and offer him temporary refuge. If this bitter mythological battle of the sexes has roots in Aristophanes, Abell carries its implications well beyond those of the classical paradigm. Mankind is in this play the master of the gods, for gods and goddesses are conceived of merely as "a collection of castoff thoughts" which man once thought and has now forgotten. "But the thread is not yet severed—not quite" (15), and hence they live on in a dreary eternity of crumbling marble ruins. (The "atmosphere of dignified but decorative decay" in this dusty symbol world was vividly concretized in the extraordinary surrealistic design which Helge Refn created for the production.)

"Zeus and his gang," who never actually appear in the play, are described as a self-seeking band of ugly, wizened manipulators of power whose leader bears every resemblance to Sartre's crafty god of the flies and death. Compromise is their watchword: "They want peace at any price, with everything and everyone—even with those clouds they ought to hate openly because they imply the destruction of other clouds," Hera, wife of Zeus, declares. "They indulge only in a little verbal hatred and always behind closed doors—that way it's done without disrupting their alibi. It would be irresponsible, no matter how much right one had, to run any kind of risk" (31).[10] Opposed to them are the goddesses and the positive values for which they stand: Aphrodite (love), Eos (light), Demeter (fertility), and Hera (marriage).

The nameless flyer, the potential new Adam who will smash the old image of Jovian man, quickly finds himself the focus of this epic conflict. "The neglected, starved goddesses sense the man's presence like a stream of warm light through space," writes Brix in his review. Christened Icarus by them, he will provide them with the means of dragging the gods down "from the blue trapezes of eternity" by force:

Yes, Icarus. He is our answer. He is the direction they have forgotten. Now we can point it out, show them the answer. Look at mankind today, at how far they have progressed down there. *Look at him.* Then *look at us,* a stone herbarium of old thoughts. *He* brings us new life. With his help this cloud shall again drop anchor, life shall again win out over marble. We have waited long, Aphrodite, but now victory is at hand, our victory—woman's victory! (32)

The second act closes on a much less optimistic note. Aphrodite's efforts to reach Icarus have failed. Crippled by his own sense of guilt and despair, he remains impervious to her influence. "That which we wanted—that hope you have taken from us. Tonight you will stand face to face with the old gods," she warns him as the ominous drums of Zeus and his destructive forces draw nearer:

Hear Zeus! He is on the way! *(Distant fanfares are heard.)* Now he marches along the marble pathways of the cloud to meet mankind. He will meet you, and he will see himself as in a mirror. The clothes of course are a little strange, he will think, but clothes are something one can overlook. The naked man is the same old image of man. He will be delighted and will stretch out his noble hand toward you, you will take it and look into his kindly eyes, see the power that is not felt as power. . . . You're their friend, after all, they need you. Without you where would their power be? It is their game you are playing. They will transform your defeat to victory—to a victory for themselves. (66)

Symbolically, the coming of Zeus is also the approach of a death which the nameless protagonist can embrace or reject. Only at the very close of the play, as the menacing drums of the god threaten to overwhelm Olympus, does this conflict reach a resolution. Overcoming the doubt and guilt which, in Abell as much as in Sartre or Nietzsche, perpetuate Zeus's power over man, He chooses to live. In this existential choice lies the seeds of victory for Aphrodite's cause.

Among the goddesses themselves, meanwhile, a level of intramural tensions is also developed, in which the human interloper again functions as a catalytic agent. His unexpected arrival literally transforms and revivifies not only the barren grey cloudscape of Olympus, but also the very personality of its aging queen. "Ah, bird," cries Aphrodite as the flyer's aircraft drones above her temple, "your battle cry makes me young again, the many years have slipped away from me. Look me in the eyes if you dare! See who I am! A queen upon a cloud" (19).

Before her daughter's eyes Aphrodite's dress changes color, her
eyes change expression, and "suddenly the air is filled with—is it
music? Yes, harps—everything is flowering, there are flowers
everywhere. Mother—you're not my mother any longer—you're
young!" (23). Perceiving the restoration ("one can see at a glance
that you're in your working clothes") the autocratic *hausfrau* Hera
and her more retiring companion Demeter diplomatically lay aside
old hostilities to form a defense alliance with the love goddess. In
the past, Aphrodite's former erotic prowess ("My love was a bonfire!
Every breath a flame!") has caused Demeter and her respectable
domestic sisters to "give her temple a wide berth" (51). Now, however, her powers of tender persuasion are seen as indispensable in
bringing Icarus to their side in the war against Zeus.

The concept of love is, however, dealt with in a far more involved
manner in Abell's fantastic theater of the mind than this last remark
might suggest. Aphrodite is no mere Circean temptress. The sen-
sual and slightly ridiculous seduction scene which she prepares in
the second act ("the whole boudoir decked out against the
background of a thunderstorm—harps and flowers—and feminine
stupidity" (60)) is inevitably an embarrassing failure. In fact, Aphrodite's power is greatly diminished in this fragmented and downcast
universe—illustrated in the curious trichotomy of her traditional
personality which the play establishes. It is, at least one critic has
argued, "this divinity's inner conflict which constitutes the true
substance of the work."[11] In dramatic terms this inner conflict is
expressed through the presence of two characters of Abell's own
invention, Anadyomene and Kokyta. In Greek mythology the name
Anadyomene ("the person born out of the foam of the sea") is one
given to Aphrodite herself, but here she is the goddess's daughter,
half human and half divine, young and surging with life's potential.
Kokyta, a former harlot of renown, is now Aphrodite's decrepit old
maidservant. She is the Great Whore, a grotesque and debased
image of human love "doomed to an eternal life on the cloud for
having boasted, in order to boost her own business, that she was of
divine origin."[12] This triad personifies the triple nature of love in
Days on a Cloud: Aphrodite is mature and maternal love, Anadyomene embodies youthful, innocent love, and Kokyta represents
love as an object to be bought and sold.

The working out of Icarus's salvation is linked directly to all three
of these representative figures. The restless Anadyomene, the

paradox in whom "the earthly and the divine struggle," falls swiftly in love with the mortal guest, and struggles bitterly against the imagined competition which her newly rejuvenated mother offers in this regard. "But she will never succeed—never. From now on I'll let my nails grow—to claws!" (28) When the parachutist's aircraft is sighted at the beginning of the play, the young Anadyomene senses that "life is beginning—my life" and adds eagerly: "Ah, Icarus from earth—take me with you!" (17) The male object of this passionate erotic rivalry remains indifferent, however, and the daughter becomes convinced that her mother has betrayed her ("I knelt and prayed to the goddess of love, but she will not surrender love"). Impetuously she runs out into the storm caused by Zeus, and is struck down by the god's thunderbolt. Her death becomes the sacrifice that Aphrodite must offer to save Icarus—a sacrifice which, as the goddess is brought to realize, represents "a much greater love" than the merely physical or selfish. The dying Anadyomene is thus able to persuade Icarus to face life again, and she follows him back to earth "as a thought—our thought." Kokyta's sneering wisecrack as she watches the parachutist descend—"He's floating. He will always float. I know him and mankind. Everything stays the same." (83)— quickly seals her fate. This deformed and sharp-tongued creature ("a grey rat she seemed, greedy, nimble, pointy-nosed, and with noticeable remnants of the walk and grace of her profession" in Clara Pontoppidan's effective rendering of the role[13]) is depicted from the outset as a distorted caricature of the old Adam which Icarus will eventually destroy: "She knows that he, the new man, must smash the image of the old. She is the old image that must be smashed" (33). Her final annihilation by the will of Hera is thus the inevitable consequence of Aphrodite's victory and of the symbolic redemption of the protagonist. Of the original triad Aphrodite alone remains, restored to her full and indivisible divinity: "Were I chosen again today to be goddess of love, I would say: yes. For ye heavens, how the earth needs to be in love!" (82)

The empyrean conflicts and metaphysical tensions generated in the play's "heavenly" sphere are complemented, meanwhile, but another distinct level of action which concerns the more down-to-earth causes surrounding the scientist's attempted suicide—which he has tried to camouflage as an accident resulting from barometric experiments he has undertaken. Once in each of the play's three acts, one of two earthly witnesses against him are mysteriously summoned by the goddesses and appear spotlighted in a kind of psychoanalytic flashback. The first of these "realistic" figures (like the character of He, neither has a name) is the neglected and rebellious Wife; the other is the shadowy character of a young girl whose brother has been killed in the war after having been inspired to join the Resistance movement by a well-sounding but since forgotten speech the scientist once made. This aspect of the play—the more personal drama of the disillusioned flyer's vain attempt to flee his human responsibilities through self-destruction—is thematically yoked to the conflicts on Olympus by means of a recurring metaphor. Its point lies in the contrast which the playwright draws between the proverbially ineffectual drop in the ocean (or the bucket, as the case may be) and the crucial last drop which causes the cup to run over. In the heavenly sphere, Aphrodite's critical decision to play her part in the campaign of the goddesses against Zeus, regardless of the sacrifice involved, is prompted by Eos's sudden adoption of this image:

EOS.   You always talk about two drops. The one adds nothing to a sea—the other makes a cup overflow. The first is the dream of revolt, the second the will to concrete action. To you, both drops are empty figures of speech—never drops of blood.
APHRODITE.   They are, Eos—they are! . . . I shall fight *(Anadyomene's laughter is heard)*—and I shall believe! . . . You didn't force me. The drop forced me. I was born of the sea—of the sea foam. Now I am reborn of a drop.

(54–55)

Not many minutes later in the second act, the Sister, who appears in a flashback to confront the protagonist with his own cowardly failure to live up to the philosophy of activism which he so glibly preached to her dead brother, returns to the same metaphor in her accusation:

You opened his eyes. You made him a living human being. You gave him the faith to believe that a drop—even the smallest—is never just a drop in the ocean. . . . He hated force, he hated injustice. But justice—can it ever be achieved if we are so fearful of doing injustice that we dare not move at all, dare not set sail for fear of underwater reefs? Have we the right to live today on such a distant Olympus—? (63–64)

This metaphor is a succinct image of the moral conflict which rages within Icarus himself. Once able to convince someone else that even the smallest drop is never *just* a drop in the sea, he has drawn back from the implications of that faith. No longer able to accept that "bitter truth" of Nordahl Grieg's, that "good can only survive through force," he has betrayed himself by taking refuge in defensive self-righteousness and "a clear conscience." The confrontation with the Sister has broken through these defenses and has been the ostensible psychological reason for his desperate flight; in these terms, her contemptuous remark about "a distant Olympus" explains why he imagines himself on Aphrodite's cloud as he plunges through the air. At the end of the play, the renewed sense of belongingness and solidarity which He reaches during his days on a cloud is once again expressed in the guise of the drama's recurrent motif: "Even if I should founder again—it will not matter. I know now that I am a drop in that ocean on which mankind will one day sail free" (83).

The character of the Wife, the other witness summoned by the goddesses to confront the disheartened scientist, appears in the first act with a brief, conventional denunciation of his neglect and loss of vitality ("You're already dead. I'm married to a dead man"). In the final act, however, she returns to deliver an immense emotional tirade which starts by developing on these personal, domestic complaints and ultimately explodes in a blistering universal indictment of the irresponsibility and "democratic humanitarianism" of scientists in general. From being a fighter, she argues, her husband has become a passive adherent of compassionate compromise: "An apostle could not have his pockets more full of forgiveness." From a fearless spokesman for his own convictions, he has turned into a silent, embittered model of blameless conduct: "Always that struggle—that theoretical struggle for a clear conscience." As a scientist, his smugly detached, ethereal notion of "freedom" causes him to float above society: "there where the air becomes thin and pale blue, there they float, society's flowers": "The spirit is free, without restraint. We know that. But why don't you stay up there in your celestial spheres where we can watch you—admire you? Why don't you leave the rest of us in peace?" (77–78). But instead, she continues passionately, science was not content until it had penetrated to the very core of life and of death. Obediently and unconditionally, without ever "allowing mankind to find its own answer," they handed over the atomic weapon to "the politicians who gave the order": "—as one orders a cream cake from the confectioner's. Yours was a poisoned cake. You knew, but you accepted the order. The spirit is free, without restraint. Rather die than abandon the principle of freedom. Rather let others die. Us! All of us!" (78). Instead of setting the final period to war, however, the bomb has become merely a comma—and the scientists must bear full responsibility for the hell of the following clause. "You gave away the weapon, the knowledge, everything—and showed us that freedom, freedom without restraint, can lead straight to the suicide of humanity," she cries (79).

Filled with much more passion than logic, the Wife's long, angry oration (virtually a monologue) has frequently invited overemphasis. One may, of course, well imagine its impact on a theater audience in 1947. It brought down the house in the young Bodil Kjer's vigorous performance—but it also brought down over its author's head the wrath of those who saw in it an ideological rejection of the Western powers and their atomic might (before Russia developed its own nuclear capacity in 1949) and even as a defense of "the Soviet Union's totalitarian state system."[14] From another standpoint entirely, Schyberg's review called it the drama's "warmest and strongest speech," adding that it "turns the play in its last act from the realm of the abstract to that of the humanly and theatrically concrete." Both views tend, for different reasons, to overstate the centrality of this much-discussed passage. In dramatic terms, the Wife's appearance becomes a contributing though not decisive factor in the outcome of the struggle being waged for her husband's salvation. (Since he is evidently a medical scientist who worked in a hospital during the war, the relevance of her attack to his case is not even fully apparent.) As for political considerations, the entire play is conceived as an expressive image of a fragmented world picture, for which the atomic bomb simply provides a historical context.[15]

At the center of *Days on a Cloud* is the interior drama of Icarus himself. The suicidal plunge of the central character not only provides a framework for the dramatic action—it *is* the dramatic action insofar as the play's vision is an expressionistic one, a projection of his mental processes. The struggle taking place within this anonymous modern Everyman during the fleeting seconds of his fall is projected externally in the guise of the characters and events of the play. On this level, his perspective is the controlling one. Hence all of the work's intersecting planes of tension—the clash between the goddesses and the forces of Zeus, the conflict within Aphrodite herself, the sacrifice and fate of Anadyomene, the more personal accusations of the Wife and the Sister—converge and are resolved in his final decision to return to life. Beneath the play's metaphysical ambiguities and shimmering obscurities, the fundamental significance of this decision is readily apparent. It reflects the familiar Abellian polarization between an open and a closed response to life. Self-destruction, a solution humorously denied Larsen in *The Melody that Got Lost* and considered only in passing by Mirena in *The Queen on Tour,* has now become a very real alternative—the terrible consequence of the isolation, apathy, and escapism with which Abell is increasingly concerned in his later plays. In its rejection of social passivity and its earnest plea for active resistance to injustice, *Days on a Cloud* aligns itself with the playwright's earlier work, especially *Anna Sophie Hedvig* and *Judith.* However, both its tighter focus on the existential crisis of the alienated individual and the structural innovations which this new focus brings with it are signposts of the future, indicators of the direction Abell's writing would follow after 1950.

II *Incidental Music*

"I believe in implacability. All who think and who work after us must know that there is only one defense against fear and dread: humanity's implacable attitude toward injustice." This characteristic Abellian declaration might well have found a place in *Days on a Cloud;* in fact, it is spoken by the Lady of the House in Abell's short festival play *Ejendommen Matr. Nr. 267 Østre Kvarter (Lot No. 267 East District),* written to commemorate the bicentennial of the Danish Royal Theater in 1948. This charming trifle is otherwise unencumbered by earnest moral issues, however, and it reflects its author in his most relaxed and genial mood, at ease in his singer's robes. Throughout his career, Abell remained (paradoxically?) the master of the well-turned occasional piece. The closing of Dagmar Theater (1937), the opening of Tivoli's new Concert Hall (1956), the New Theater's fiftieth jubilee (1958), and many similar public occasions were enhanced by a graceful prologue or epilogue from his prolific pen.[16] As the official eulogist for the Royal Theater's two-hundredth birthday, he was also the ideal choice. A remarkable sixteen-day festival of plays and ballets was prepared for the bicentenary of Scandinavia's oldest state theater on December 18, 1948, and on the day itself Abell's engaging *tour de force* contributed a satisfying apotheosis. His tribute took the form of a one-act potpourri of familiar scenes and popular moments from the Royal Theater repertory, set to music by Knudåge Riisager and acted by a once-in-a-lifetime cast headed by Poul Reumert and Bodil Ipsen, as the Master and the Lady of the House. This poetic bagatelle is charged with Abell's view of the theater as "the free imagination's fantastic sanctuary" in which "everything relies upon the word, the word's determination never to let itself be bought"—a theater of infinite possibilities, aimed at provoking the spectator into seeking his own solutions. In a scene between the Dark Hostess (Melpomene) and the Light Hostess (Thalia), the latter tells a window washer who has found his way into this magical world: "They divided us up into two answers, a 'yes' and a 'no,' two answers to life. But we are not answers! Only questions. We ask—you must answer."[17] *Theater Sketches in Easter Weather*, the little book of theatrical impressions ("spontaneous selections from memoirs never to be written," Abell calls it) which appeared in the same year as *Lot 267*, is filled with the same insistence on an engaged and "creative" audience and the same despair over "the passive spectator" whose "creative imagination has long since been forced into an amiable but tighter and tighter straightjacket."[18]

Less than three months after his festival play, on February 13, 1949, the Royal Theater was ready to unveil yet another new work by Abell, entitled *Miss Plinckby's kabale (Miss Plinckby's Solitaire)*. This time, however, audiences and critics who may have come prepared for his usual arguments and earnest remonstrances were confronted with a curious anomaly—a rather inconsequential three-act comedy which, as the dramatist readily acknowledged, represented recreational therapy after the rigors of *Days on a Cloud*. "Interdium dormitat bonus Homerus," Schyberg declared indulgently, invoking Horace's testimony that even Homer himself sometimes slept, and went on to characterize Abell's new play as "a graceful and very capricious game."[19] Other reviewers were less tolerant of what *Berlingske Tidende* called "the elevated, gas-blue, and triple-starred atmosphere" of this sophisticated drawing-room comedy, "where intellect and dream intertwine fingers to the cultivated accompaniment of tinkling champagne glasses and piano strings."[20] The work of Noël Coward immediately comes to mind as an obvious prototype for the experiment; the play is, however, also very similar in theme and technique to Abell's own films from the early forties, in particular "Thanks for Coming, Nick." Though its dialogue does not compare very favorably with the restrained and sharply honed wit of Coward, *Miss Plinckby's Solitaire* benefited on the stage from the performances of such masters of the elegant conversation piece as Reumert, Bodil Ipsen, and Mogens Wieth. ("There *are* times when one is almost vexed," Brix remarked acidly, "by the incredible power of theater art to do all the work for a Mister Voltisubito"[21])

The slight comic intrigue which Abell sets in motion follows well-worn paths. Herbert and Constance, bourgeois archetypes both, are trapped in a conventional and uninspired marriage which is, by now, devoid of meaning and suffocated by business duties and social routines. Herbert, says his bored, frustrated, and introverted wife, "is just a tuxedo, a correct tuxedo," fond of playing solitaire and addicted to wearing suspenders "both spiritually and physically."[22] "The whole thing is kept going," says he of the marital state, "by sheer contrariness. If one is sullen, the other smiles—and vice versa. When one is down, the other immediately rushes skyward. We meet only for an instant—each in his passing elevator. More it never amounts to" (70). Laura, worldly-wise family friend, translator of cheap fiction, and the play's most vigorous and most entertaining character, strives vainly to introduce a breath of fresh air into their unenthusiastic and tedious existence.

True to the familiar formula, the first-act curtain is brought down on a complicating (if somewhat unlikely) development. At midnight on an enchanting midsummer eve (Barrie's kind of night, rather than Strindberg's), a mysterious "young man from across the way" whom Laura and Constance have previously been ogling from the latter's penthouse terrace arrives at the door to demand admittance. His presence in the play is given an explanation of the flimsiest, offstage variety: Constance, meeting him downstairs at a mailbox and observing his hesitation at posting a letter, has impulsively seized his epistle and tossed it into the box. Proclaiming that she has thereby taken his destiny into her hands and that he will stay with her forever, the enigmatic and handsome stranger has pursued the terrified Constance to her apartment. Here he is found at the beginning of the second act, firmly ensconced and dreamily playing the adagio movement from Beethoven's Pathétique Sonata! A dramatic catalyst if ever there was one. Methodically he exposes the superficialities of this affluent bourgeois milieu—"rooms that are never lived in, books that are never read [the play abounds in bookish allusions to Balzac, Dostoevski, Stendhal, Defoe, D. H. Lawrence, and Dickens], days that pass without event," as Schyberg writes in his review. "Urges not obeyed through fear of what one can or cannot do, and of what 'others' might say. People who stagnate and wither because they have lost all spontaneity in their relation to life." Although Michael, as the young man chooses to call himself, at one point even uses the word "suicide" to characterize this undeniably bleak mentality, the general tone of Abell's comedy is blandly urbane and ironic, occasionally maudlin but always well-bred. Inspired by the June night, vast quantities of alcohol, and Michael's attractive nonchalance and tall tales of exotic adventure, the others are drawn into the spirit of this elegant *clownerie*. The ensuing fun and games are cerebral, never visceral, and antiseptically bloodless (such indelicate pastimes as humping the hostess and getting the guest were yet to be invented). A rejuvenated Herbert is taught a brand-new way of playing his solitaire by the charming visitor—originally devised by a shadowy and possibly fictitious Peruvian governess named Miss Plinckby; the boys playfully prepare an elaborate midnight supper, and then conclude the second act with a high-spirited wrestling match on the living-room floor.

As the dawn breaks and "a bird suddenly begins to twitter" outside, the final act neatly resolves all problems—and in so doing destroys any dramatic tension which has accumulated around the enigmatic intruder. This fascinating stranger from across the world turns out to be a quite ordinary young man who lives with his red-haired and pregnant wife across the street. To make matters worse, the letter which Constance so impetuously tossed into the mailbox proves to be neither more nor less than Michael's idealistic refusal of a job offer as director of exports in Herbert's company! ("I have always loved my freedom. Could I renounce it? I could not, I can not," he explains, without the slightest trace of irony.) This rather nebulous character, in many ways a less successful comic parallel to Anna Sophie Hedvig, is generally lacking in the purposefulness and clarity of definition that make Anna a dramatic force to be reckoned with. Although efforts are continually made to surround him with an air of mystery and strength ("From the first moment I caught that quick little glint in his eyes, I knew that he was a tourist from another world"), the trite social reality to which his enigmatic presence is ultimately reduced robs the comedy of subtlety. "To gain admission to these heavens, one sells his freedom for the highest bid," Laura admonishes him with melodramatic fervor: "One pretends to himself that he is selling something external, something that doesn't matter, is unessential—until one day he realizes that he has sold himself—and the sale is final" (97). Strengthened in his resolve to avoid the snares of gainful employment, "Michael" returns to his bohemian "world" across the street. The others, we are asked to believe, have also learned from this midsummer-night's encounter session, for they have "suddenly seen their world as he has seen it." Herbert, the erstwhile "tuxedo," seems particularly changed in his outlook ("Laura, this isn't a home, this here—but a prison. These bookcases—everywhere there are galleries with cells, in every cell an innocent prisoner sits moping"), and as the curtain falls, he is seen gently teaching Constance the rudiments of Miss Plinckby's mystical game of solitaire.

Like *Lot 267*, *Miss Plinckby's Solitaire* demonstrates the playwright's keen practical sense of the abilities of the leading Royal Theater players to whom these pieces were tailored. Both plays can be classed as pleasant "incidental music" within the larger context of Abell's work. Despite its relative lack of artistic significance, however, *Plinckby* deserves mention as a transitional work in which a principal line of thematic development in Abell's later plays is present in embryo. Schyberg, alone among the play's reviewers, attempted to describe the serious thematic undertone which plays beneath the contrived surface of this curiously flawed comedy, and which links it to the darker dramas which follow (but which Schyberg never lived to see): "Regardless of how much we hate and despise one another, how much we are enemies and opponents, and are weary of one another or combat one another . . . we are nonetheless related to, and share the same earth with, one another. And there are moments when we sense this. Brief moments, but they do exist—when we can greet our strange fellow creatures with a smile, and wish that we ordinarily understood one another a little better."

"A toast," cries the new-born Herbert boisterously, "a toast for the lilies of the field and the birds of the air—and a toast for the moment in which we live."

III   Vetsera *(1950)*

By the time Kjeld Abell's three-act chamber play, *Vetsera blomstrer ikke for enhver* (*Vetsera Does Not Bloom for Everyone*), opened at the intimate Frederiksberg Theater on November 12, 1950, its author had departed on a trip to India which marked the first of several pilgrimages to the Far East. By the time he returned to Denmark, his new play, which met with critical and box-office failure at its first performance, had long since closed. Abell's journey to India, which culminated in a meeting with Pandit Nehru, is the subject of his vivid travel book *Fodnoter i Støvet* (*Footnotes in the Dust*, published 1951). In this sensitive volume of impressions, the playwright's initial encounter with "an Asia that in size and strength can cause all measuring sticks to break into bits and pieces" emerges as an experience which profoundly affected and broadened his outlook. In an interesting sense this little travel book complements the forebodingly somber *Vetsera*, by casting the play's picture of a decadent and dying Western culture into the broader perspective of the awakening East's problems and challenges. In *Vetsera*, Abell holds final judgment over a sterile world "where despair is the leitmotiv, where sincerity has been transformed into social games, and from which tenderness has been banished."[23] "Far from here, infinitely far," writes Abell himself in *Footnotes in the Dust*, in a passage that offers a noteworthy contrast to the wasteland images of withered vegetation and lifeless ice flowers which proliferate in *Vetsera*, "a pair of feet walk a roadside of dust, walk as though they alone knew what it means: to walk, to walk like an uprooted flower which still continues to bloom."[24] The implied dichotomy—between the fecundity and movement of life, and the barrenness and stagnant decay of an existence that shuts out life—is at the core of Abell's darkest and most elusive play.

Its title and its theme play obliquely upon the facts and obscurities surrounding the well-known double suicide of the baroness Maria Vetsera and crown prince Rudolph of Austria, son of the emperor Franz Joseph, at the hunting lodge of Mayerling in 1889. On a January morning in that year, the neurotic Archduke Rudolph and his mistress were discovered shot to death; a double suicide pact was a foregone conclusion—Maria Vetsera lay covered with flowers, while her lover, who had killed himself some hours later, still held the pistol in his hand. A number of plays and films have, of course, dealt with the mysterious Hapsburg tragedy (including Maxwell Anderson's typically political interpretation of it, entitled *The Masque of Kings*). Abell's *Vetsera*, however, is concerned only very indirectly with the actual historical event, which serves as a suggestive and recurring background referent in the drama. An earlier draft of the play apparently stems from the same period as his *Judith*— a work to which it bears some resemblance in the depiction of a central female character who resists the imposition of her historical namesake's fate upon her. Otherwise, however, the interplay of past and present is treated very differently in *Vetsera*, in which no attempt is made to bring history onto the stage. Its characters are wholly contemporary, as representative of a doomed society as are the inhabitants of Bernard Shaw's *Heartbreak House*.

Affinities between Abell's drama and Shaw's bitter apocalyptic masterpiece are, in fact, numerous. One might even inscribe *Vetsera* with Shaw's famous subtitle, "a fantasia in the Russian manner." The manner alluded to is Chekhovian, and the dictionary definition of a fantasia (an instrumental composition, seemingly extemporaneous, "in which form is subservient to fancy") implies clearly enough the deliberate sense of indirection and nonsequentiality, the carefully concealed plotting, noninterlocking dialogue, and dramatic pointillism of a Chekhov play. Each character, glimpsed, as it were, in a series of fleeting impressions, appears absorbed in his own monodrama. Communication in the usual sense seems absent, while a strong subtext of unstated meanings runs beneath and between the lines that are actually spoken. In its best moments, during its first two acts, *Vetsera* touches the Chekhovian method which Shaw also emulates (and modifies) in *Heartbreak House*. Other aspects of Abell's play are similarly "Chekhovian" in flavor: the crumbling country estate, and the inevitable pattern of arrival-sojourn-departure; the weave of frustrated or unrealized love affairs which holds the ostensible "plot" together; above all, the pungent mood of spiritual weariness and paralysis, undercut occasionally by the intrusion of a farcical or absurd element (represented in this case by the antics of the voluble Pastor Panne). Like Shaw (and unlike Chekhov), meanwhile, Abell passes judgment on his characters and on the society they represent; neither playwright had much "faith in these charming people extricating themselves," as Shaw put it in his

Preface. That the relative scope of this judgment is much diminished in Abell seems almost self-evident—the conflagration which ends his play is bound to seem but a tinkle compared to the thunderous Armageddon which Shaw brings down upon his Heartbreak House.

Perhaps the most forceful "character" in *Vetsera* is the setting itself, the pseudo-classical country estate which commands the stage and embodies in its atmosphere of stagnation the suffocating weight of a dead past. By implication, it projects an image of an outmoded cultural pattern which has lost its justification and its meaning (just as Heartbreak House "is cultured, leisured Europe before the [first] war"). Decay is everywhere, "but a decay that has stopped. Even for a moth there is nothing more left to devour."[25] The play's effectiveness in the theater depends heavily on the stage designer's ability to "sense this atmosphere and come implicitly to terms with it," as art historian Christian Elling wrote in an unusual little review of the set itself, created by Helge Refn. "Everything is ominous, ambiguous, like figures in a tarnished mirror or like an interrupted dream," Elling continues, and both Refn's stylized exterior ("slender pillars form a little stage-within-the-stage, with a striped awning for a roof") and his overheated Strindbergian "conservatory" with its moldering flowers and crumbling furniture lent an almost tangible concreteness to the incorporeal mood of dream and decay.[26] In a mystical sense, this death house bears the sinister name of Mayerling:

ALICE.   The house could have been given many names. Mayerling was the most decorative.

HENRY.   Was it in conversation that he gave the house that name?

VETSERA.   No, it's written on the pillars by the drive.

ALICE.   And on the frontispiece facing the garden. Odd that you never saw it.

VETSERA.   I never saw it either.

HENRY.   Oh, now didn't you really.

VETSERA.   Because it was always dark when we came, and—he always turned in from the road so suddenly that I sat with my life in my hands. But he described the letters. Even though letters seem to me somehow strange to describe. I suppose it was because one or the other of his grandparents had set them up. That's how I understood it.

ALICE.   Now they have all been taken down. Toward the garden anyway.

BOB.   Also toward the road—I would imagine.
ALICE.   Only the light impressions remain on the dark sandstone—and
the black holes from the wall brackets.
HENRY.   Now listen here. . . .

                                                                    (39–40)

The curiously brittle and unreal conversation, itself so characteristic of the general tone of the work, refers to the house's dead
owner David, whose burial has just been completed when the play
begins. He is its unseen protagonist, and his alcoholic self-
destruction presents an emotionally cold and even banal contrast to
the romantic Mayerling motif which he has tried unsuccessfully to
emulate. His deserted and cheerless house, a museum of dead objects that have "stolen their owner's face," is a living image of his
alienated, unfree personality. Only the cathartic destruction of the
house at the close of the play can end the spell of barren futility
which David seems to have cast on those around him.
    It is, then, the telling of David's story—a story which, director
Edwin Tiemroth insisted in a radio interview before the first production, was meant to be "taken as it is experienced, not translated
into symbols"—which constitutes the main "action" in this essentially actionless, retrospective drama. The play's structure is thus
static and "contextual," focusing on time-stopped moments of
chorded experience rather than on the linear progression of conventional drama. In the course of this tightly compressed chamber
play's three brief acts, which span the time from late afternoon until
near midnight on the day of David's funeral, bits and pieces of the
past emerge and coalesce like the fragments of an intricate jigsaw
puzzle. (That this complex and sometimes symbol-clogged process
places unusually heavy demands on an audience in the theater is
incontrovertible; to Schyberg's successor Harald Engberg, the original production seemed "unquestionably more philosophy than
play, more puzzle than poetry. If one lacks a brain like a can opener,
he will not belong among the chosen few to whom the poet's king-
dom will be revealed."[27])
    As the various characters who arrive at David's fictive Mayerling
on his burial day talk and soliloquize about the past, the contours of
his wasted life gradually become clear. Here as in his related plays
(Days on a Cloud, The Blue Pekinese), suicide is for Abell the ultimate negation, the fearful consequence of self-inflicted isolation and
alienation from humanity. David, the egoist and esthete whose

"favorite pastime was at all costs to be unusual," has discovered too late that his intellectual isolationism will revenge itself, that the role he adopts can become irreversible: "He became lonely because he believed he was alone. At last he was alone because others took him at his word and respected his need for aloneness. He became so alone that—the rest had to be Mayerling. The final twist in his protest against himself" (43). Ironically, however, this escapist's last desperate pretence—to stage a pleasingly arranged suicide together with a Vetsera who would provide "the final flourish before he was relegated as a topic of conversation to—emptiness" (59)—has failed, and he has been left to die in solitude.

"David? David was crazy," reasons his insensitive brother and alter ego Henry, a stolid and overbearing businessman stereotype who, as his wife Alice retorts, would "never stop to draw his own normality into question." This no less hollow and isolated individual fails utterly to perceive the meaning of David's fate or its possible relevance to himself:

ALICE.   That pale little snapshot of the two of you as boys in on your mother's windowsill, the one where you're as alike as two drops of water, both in short pants and on a pair of skinny legs, you know the one.
HENRY.   Yes. What about it?
ALICE.   It's not the sun that has faded it. In the course of the years it has simply turned paler and paler in its surprise at seeing how differently the same family recipe can turn out.
HENRY.   Rubbish.
ALICE.   Yes. Everything is rubbish. It's just such a sorry result to come to. Don't you think?

(15–16)

Their mordant exchanges in the first act are interrupted, in true Chekhovian fashion, by the almost slapstick intrusion of the distracted Pastor Panne in search of water for his boiling automobile. However, the ground has been prepared for their rather predictable confrontation and marital breakup at the end of the long night of revelations.

Alice, one more Abellian "widow" whose empty marriage to Henry has made her "an ice flower on the windowpane" that separates her from life, is more self-analytical than her stuffy husband, and hence more responsive to the significance of David's tragedy. Her love for him shines through her very first speech, the evocative eulogy she recites as she enters slowly from the garden at the beginning of the play:

One should always come from the garden—you used to say. Up over the lawn, past the sundial and the magnolia that your grandfather cut down. A little way from the house you would stop and see yourself as a small boy in the family gathering between the pillars. I, too, can see you. I see your eyes. They want to escape, get away, but know they cannot. Now they're gone. And you are gone. *(Walks to a small round garden table standing beside one of the pillars.)* David. Your funeral, the way you had wanted it, left me cold, ice cold. But here by the table before the pillars I will hold my farewell speech. No speech, for I have nothing to say. The poems you once gave me I place here. At the front you wrote: For Alice. Beneath it I have written: For David. (10)

Although the entire play elapses before the nature of their relationship becomes clear, the repeated references to the flowering magnolia they replanted in the garden and to the volume of David's verses ("highly peculiar poems" in the opinion of the ubiquitous Panne, who acquires them by accident but reads them voraciously before returning them) are attempts to suggest its fragile, curiously self-conscious quality. Together, they acted out David's private game of uniqueness, of pretended superiority to the common human cycle of birth, flowering, and death: "The others are in the majority, yet we sit in the midst of our churchyards and let on as if we were so. We are brought flowers, but we do not flower, not for everyone, only when we have found it expedient." They came together in despair, Alice finally tells us, and despair became their leitmotiv. "It was serious, but the seriousness was transformed into a party game" (63). She *was* David's imaginary Vetsera, until she realized the true purpose of his games—"to die, to take his own life, he was only capable of it at the top of a game. His vanity was so boundless that he was unable to do it alone, he could not die in the solitude which he himself had created" (59). Instinctively, she laughed—"self-preservation's unarticulated answer to absurdity"[28]—and fled. Only the "real" Vetsera, however, the young girl in grey whom Bob, the bland family lawyer, brings with him to the house and whom Alice almost clairvoyantly greets as "David's heir," has the power to release her from his dead, paralyzing influence.

The second act belongs to the shadowy and reticent Vetsera, who in a sense holds the key to the play's mystery. A strong subtext of suspicion and double meanings runs beneath the apparently trivial surface of the after-dinner conversation in the oppressive grey conservatory, the room where David had twice tried to stage his distorted Mayerling pastiche. His second attempt was with Vetsera herself, a very ordinary, frightened young girl whose (fortuitously coincidental) name alone has drawn him to her, as a convenient device with which to invest his own death with artificial meaning. Dazzled by his wealth and eloquence, it seemed to her that "the walls opened, the ceiling became the sky, and we danced under the great chandeliers that hung beneath the stars"—the resonances from Anouilh's great success *Léocadia,* even called *Dance Under the Stars* in Danish and staged by Edwin Tiemroth three months before Abell's play opened, seem too strong to be overlooked. The fable is reversed, however, for this grey girl of the people stands no chance of overcoming the prince's self-deceptive illusions. Reluctantly, she recognizes David for what he was:

HENRY.   He was sick.
VETSERA.   No! He was a criminal. A frigid, perverted criminal. He wanted only one thing. To die. But not alone. . . .

(37)

She, too, has rejected the fate which he and her own name have endeavored to impose upon her. "Vetsera, said my sister—Vetsera does not bloom for everyone, she blooms suddenly, in a single night. That is Vetsera's destiny, said David. Vetsera's destiny. I never understood either of them."

Even the name itself is a grim practical joke that life has played on her. Given it by an ambitious mother who thought it "elegant" and never realized it was a surname, it has lent her a false, unwelcome attractiveness which her constrained, unresponsive personality could not sustain. ("I have always—felt cold. I have always longed for warmth, but have always become frightened when anyone showed me warmth.") Humiliated by her sister's profession—she is a prostitute whom Henry has frequented (has she perhaps even prompted Vetsera's dangerous liaison with David for reasons of potential personal profit?)—and intimidated by David's family, she remains watchful and defensive in the unfamiliar milieu, holding fast to the blank check for "everything he possesses" which David has left her. "Nothing could make you break out and show yourself as a human being," Alice tells her contemptuously. "I hoped and hoped and went on hoping. But no reminiscence, no memory could subdue that petty cashier's soul which peeped out through your eyes" (34). In the course of the long night, however, the mystical bond of compassionate understanding which is forged between these two women, once they recognize David's egoistic compulsion for what it was, is able to eradicate his pernicious, life-denying influence forever.

The elusive Vetsera, in whom we might see resemblances to Chekhov's robust proletarian intruders as well as to Anouilh's restless *sauvages*, is at heart the spiritual kinswoman of those sound and vital common men who are seen to possess the melody of life in Abell's own early comedies. She represents not only the need, but also the obligation to love and to flourish. The decisive midnight conversation between her and Alice which alters their destinies is, in typical Abell fashion, neither seen nor heard by the audience. Although Vetsera herself speaks only four lines in the last act, however, her positive influence manifests itself at every turn of the action. Alice's climactic recognition that their *angst* is not produced by the fear of death, but by the "terror of dying without having lived, without having bloomed" includes Vetsera in its scope as well:

Haven't we an obligation to flower? Is that not the sole obligation we have? The question resounded like a hollow echo through the house. I heard them laughing, the dead pictures, the dead photographs. They had killed the house. Had killed all life within the house. Come—they shouted, come— will you own us and what we have owned? No. I will not own death. I will accept it as a gift—after I have lived. . . . That night I lost him. Tonight I have lost him completely. Vetsera took him from me, lifted him from my shoulders, from my conscience—and my heart. I can fly. (63–64)

It is also Vetsera who completes the enigmatic story of long-forgotten suicide which the old maidservant Mie's choral speeches have developed as a running commentary on the action—the story of David's aunt, a self-willed young girl also named Mie (that is, Marie, the historical Vetsera's first name), who took her life on her seventeenth birthday simply because she felt cheated of a dress which her parents had promised her. Like the Mayerling motif, the paradoxical story of the hapless Mie has also become a "curse," insofar as it equipped David with another neurotic fantasy on which to embroider his "hyperesthetic fretwork": "She who was never allowed to own the dress, he said—she was permitted instead to own her freedom, the only freedom worth owning. She was the first in this house, the first and the last. When she disappeared, the house became a vise from which no one could escape" (60).

In the symbolic fire which is allowed to consume this blighted house at the end of the play, all three women in the Vetsera triangle gain their freedom, as Vetsera's blank inheritance check, Alice's volume of poems, and little Mie's ghostly piano feed the flames. Vetsera's unadorned *Jo* ("yes") to Pastor Panne, when the irrepressible priest suggests "viewing the matchless spectacle" of the fire from down by the sundial, is the simplest possible reaffirmation of the drama's central theme, the ascendancy of life over the stifling forces of a lifeless and doomed past.

There are certainly internal weaknesses in *Vetsera* that are impossible to overlook, and that stand out even more prominently in the theater than in the study. The impressionistic orchestration of themes and images and the "Chekhovian" indirectness of its first two acts give way in the weak last act to an over-explicitness which critics of its first performance found anticlimactic and contrived. The windy, expository story told by Pastor Panne about his unlikely involvement on the fateful night when David nearly shot Alice is plotty and redundant. The gratuitous pairing off of the lawyer Bob, an underdeveloped and thoroughly uninteresting character, with Alice at the curtain fall is a creaky device that closes off the interest that a more open ending might otherwise hold for an audience. In the first production, moreover, the text was altered to close with an interpolated homily by Mie (Abell's Madam Helseth) to the effect that what the world needs now is love ("We must be concerned about 'ours'. But if we forget tenderness, ours becomes a shell, a house, a stone-hard rock from which neither God nor Moses can strike the smallest spring"). "It was beautifully spoken by Bodil Ipsen," commented one reviewer, "but conceived with such banality and formulated so abstractly by Abell that neither the actress's enormous personality nor Tiemroth's painstaking direction could rescue the finale."[29]

This same critic expressed a widely-held feeling that the play appears at times, especially perhaps when seen on the stage, as a veritable patchwork of borrowings from the modern repertory: "Seldom in the course of two hours has one seen such a playwrights' sampler: the Strindbergian dream play with *The Ghost Sonata;*

O'Neill's House of Atreus, casting cold shadows and with its old
retainer who, like a Greek chorus, relates forgotten episodes, recalls
the fateful family destiny, and comments on the course of events;
Anouilh's primitive girl dumped into the midst of the historical
masquerade. In the air hovers Giraudoux, as he often does in Abell,
and, finally, Ibsenian lines are dropped like sinister *bon mots.*" Not
to mention Chekhov, Shaw, and Eliot, one might add. *Vetsera* is
substantially a rebus, a labyrinth of literary anagrams and oblique
allusions to flower imagery, Mayerling, the psychologically complex
case histories of David and of little Mie, and much more. This mode
of essentially "referential" drama suggests an interesting comparison
with the poetic methods of Pound and of T. S. Eliot (whose *Wasteland* first appeared in Danish in 1948, the year of his Nobel Prize,
and may well have had some influence on Abell's play[30]). As crucial
as the referential technique has been in the evolution of modern
poetry and modern fiction, however, it remains far less well adapted
to dramatic writing. In *Vetsera,* many of its critics felt that the
playwright's meticulous attention to the references and abstractions
embedded in its dialogue led him (wrote Engberg) "to forget the
characters in whose mouths they ought to become living words. So
intently has he pondered over a meaning in his drama that his
people have ceased to interest him. . . . The fatal flaw in this production, taken as theater, is that not one of the ladies and gentlemen
on the stage really concerns us. It is like being at a party with utter
strangers."
    The verdicts handed down in 1950 were almost uniformly un-
favorable; the extent to which the fault might have lain with the
original director, cast, or audience remains a moot question. A partial answer may be suggested, however, by the popular success
which the revival of *Vetsera* enjoyed at Odense Theater in 1972, in a
production which afforded Lily Weiding (who was Vetsera in the
original production) a personal triumph as Alice, and which also
went far toward vindicating the clarity of this drama in performance.
    In general, one of the most common "interpretations" imposed on
this elusive work has been autobiographical in nature, endeavoring
in one way or another to explain or even excuse the play as a veiled
expression of a personal crisis in Abell's own life and art, a decision
on his part to "burn his own past." Such an approach sheds no useful
light on the work itself, however, and it simply inflates the artificial
myth of "obscurity" and "mystery" which has somehow attached

itself to a play that is, above all else, a rejection of all factitious mythologizing. Presumably, the writing of dramatists such as Beckett and Pinter has rendered audiences in the second half of the century less resistant to a play which, like *Vetsera*, may be not necessarily "about" something, but the very thing itself—a projection or an image of the inner human condition, to which one must respond experientially and directly. The otherwise so placid Bob is given a speech toward the end of this play which is meant to suggest the nature of the unseen communication taking place at that moment between Vetsera and Alice, but which also describes quite well that intuitive, irrational inner realm of action for which Abell tries continually in his later plays to find a means of theatrical expression:

I have a belief. In something that lies beyond visible reality. Not anything detached, looming large and threatening in the distance. I believe in the invisible bond that exists between human beings. The unexpressed which, at one and the same time, is felt as an inspiring blessing and a crushing curse. Were we able to make the unseen within us visible, then the curse would gradually lose its hold. The lonely ones would no longer need to build fortresses of their solitude. And the fortresses that exist would be demolished. Just as this house tonight—will be sold for demolition. (53)

This speech, which might well stand as a motto over all of Kjeld Abell's writing, makes explicit the idea stated in embryo in *Miss Plinckby's Solitaire*, and it also prepares us for the fuller and more consistent treatment of the theme in Abell's next play, *The Blue Pekinese*.

IV The Blue Pekinese (1954)

Perhaps, as several critics have remarked, Kjeld Abell met his oddly colored pekinese in China. The fabled blue dragon of Chinese mythology, spirit of the universe and the truth of existence, does indeed seem to share characteristics with the invisible, horizon-blue canine whose bell-tinkling presence dominates Abell's play. In 1952, the playwright and his wife visited mainland China for the first time; four years later they returned once again to the Far East, this time making the long voyage by sea from Rotterdam to Canton on board a Swedish freighter. The fictionalized record of this Chinese odyssey, entitled *De tre fra Minikoi (Three from Minikoi)* was published in 1957. It is a vivid account of Abell's fascination with the

East which abounds in impressions and reflections that also amplify the main thematic concerns of *Den blå Pekingeser (The Blue Pekinese)*.

In *Minikoi*, the traveller's response to Mao's "poem of a new China" is divided, colored strongly by his disappointed realization that art and fantasy have been pushed into the background by the overwhelming process of social and economic upheaval. Viewing a large new theater at Irkursk, for example, he is struck by the feeling that "fantasy itself, the loveliest jewel in the theater's diadem, has suddenly become homeless."[31] And yet, for Abell, the urge to dream and to fantasize (or "fabulate," as he likes to call it) can never be denied, for it is inextricably bound up with the will to life itself: "They are as supple as water, our dreams and fablings, but if one shuts them in, if one demands that the birds must sing one approved melody, only one, only one, then mountains can come crashing down and sweep everything with them" (154). Nor, he insists, is this gift of "fantasy" in any sense limited to the realm of the artist: "the ability to feel and receive inspiration lies in every man's possession" (76). By contrast, in the emotionally sterile and constricted individual—Abell's intractable widow in the mirror—the negation of this vital human ability to dream and to imagine is a manifestation of that isolation which deadens all human life.

The dichotomy between the open and the closed individual, between the "fabulist" and the petty realist, is, by now, a familiar concept in this writer's work. "The two polar opposites in his thought," observes Sven Møller Kristensen in an essay on his prose writing, "are represented by the person who has thrown up barriers around himself, and the person who lives in a pact with nature and his fellow men."[32] Hence in *Minikoi*, Bella Thornton is presented as another of "these isolated individuals" behind whose emotionally impenetrable armor hides "the completely indifferent little twelve-year-old girl who goes around alone in a big, empty house in the midst of a world that has not the least inclination to play with her" (179). The most extreme embodiment of this syndrome is Tordis Eck (Ego?) in *The Blue Pekinese*, whose isolation and threatened suicide contribute the chief source of dramatic interest in the play. The antithesis of this "hermit-crab" posture is also shown to us throughout Abell's writing in such characters as Edith, Anna Sophie Hedvig, Vetsera, the figure of John, the author's alter ego in *Minikoi*—and perhaps, by extension, in the Chinese people themselves, to whom the European cult of isolated individualism is a distinctly bourgeois and alien malady. "Only by relinquishing his individuality does one become truly liberated and thus capable of achieving fellowship with all creation," remarks one commentator who sees overtones of Eastern thought in *The Blue Pekinese;* "only then is one no longer encompassed by the narrow boundaries of the self and the ego, because he is now conscious of himself as part of a larger whole."[33] "Too late, I understood too late," Tordis Eck is similarly brought to realize in the play, "that there is a pattern, a living pattern which grows and flowers. I saw only myself, my own thread, thought that from it a pattern, an independent pattern, could be formed. A thread can easily lead one into labyrinths, but seldom out again. Now it is too late."[34] One distinct kind of contrast to Tordis's agony seems to be suggested by the vision projected in *Minikoi* of "the timeless China's fabling invisibility," the unseen pattern of Chinese life that has been formed through the centuries as a unity of nature and people (153).

It is, in fact, not "too late" for Tordis to reshape her misformed life, for her salvation in *The Blue Pekinese* is worked through the presence of living, dead, and as yet unborn characters who converge about her in this complex drama. The playwright's belief in the primacy of the imaginative sphere and in the power of that "invisible bond" to which Bob refers in *Vetsera* causes all accepted limitations of time and space, all barriers between the real and the fantastic to be set aside. Interestingly enough, meanwhile, a very comparable blurring of the contours of conventional reality pervades and enriches even so ostensibly "factual" a narrative as *Three from Minikoi.* In this novel *cum* travel book, the restless ghosts of Bella, Virginia, and Archie, dead relics of the West's decadent and discarded cultural past, board Abell's ship at Minikoi and follow the two travellers through their entire journey. Only at the very end of the book are these leprous images of the "old Adam" finally exorcized and consigned (like the decaying Villa Mayerling) to oblivion by the author. "You mean that the three existed in your mind—symbolically, so to speak?" an injudicious interviewer once asked Abell in a radio interview. "No—no, they came aboard, they *were* with us," he was heard to reply without hesitation.[35] What is implied is, of course, not spiritism, but the fabulist's inviolable privilege to render the world larger and existence more intense, to hold up to nature "that mirror which reflects not outward reality, but that which, like a vision, a network of foliage, a backbone, stands behind reality, the intangible which can only be touched at the moment of inspiration" (76). Throughout the final phase of Abell's writing runs his professed determination to confront his audience with a "brand-new, alarming world in which the livingroom's three tangible dimensions are conquered by a fourth, unknown, invisible. . . . "[36] Perhaps more strikingly than in any other later play, however, this visionary dimension is projected in *The Blue Pekinese* into theatrical terms of extraordinary scope. In this last fantasia of self-destruction, the form itself—the play's structural logic, its surreal visual effects, and its unusual dialogic method—becomes an integral function and a reflection of its central thematic conflict, the struggle between the forces of alienation and death and the power of life's unspoken and unrealized demands and potentialities.

Most first-night reviewers of the Royal Theater's production of *The Blue Pekinese* on December 16, 1954 tended (understandably enough) to bestow lavish praise on John Price's exciting mise-en-scène and on the clear, confident performances of Bodil Kjer as the dying Tordis and Mogens Wieth, returning in triumph to the Danish national stage after a five-year absence, as André, the detached spectator of life who ultimately saves her. The play itself, however, was largely overlooked as an "unclear" or even "undramatic" machinist's scenario. "Instead of writing a play, Abell has once again delivered a manuscript for a production," declared one such critic.[37] "One may think what one will of Kjeld Abell and his manner—call it poetry so personal as to be affectation, or affectation that is hard to distinguish from poetry," observed Harald Engberg from a somewhat more positive standpoint,"—it is in any case at the Royal Theater he belongs; it is there—and only there—in that immense space with its immense machinery that his numberless subterfuges can be brought to unfold like artificial flowers in the artificial light."[38] Though cognizant of this playwright's remarkable ability to exploit every aspect of the total theatrical instrument at his disposal, these opening-night notices failed manifestly to come to grips with the depth of his artistic vision—nor, in all fairness, should a theater review necessarily be expected to do so. Literary critics have generally responded more enthusiastically to the play than their practical newspaper brethren; a number have regarded it as Abell's "most controlled and disciplined work, probably on the whole his greatest achievement as a poet."[39]

Although it abounds in such typical Abell devices as flashbacks, cinematic fades, and an elaborate framework, *The Blue Pekinese* is nevertheless among his clearest and least complicated fables for the stage. Its simplicity consists in the fact that it limits itself to the exploration of a single dramatic situation, unencumbered by either the multiple plots or the frequent political, sociological, and ethical digressions of his earlier work. Once again, the situation is an existential one, hinging upon a central moment of choice. Much like the flyer in *Days on a Cloud,* Tordis Eck, shut off from the world in her lonely Villa Gullcry on the symbolically isolated and storm-lashed island of Iselø, has devised a skilfully camouflaged suicide, and hovers at the beginning of the play between life and death. Although the drama's technique also partakes of the expressionistic style of *Days on a Cloud,* however, the central character within whose consciousness the action unfolds and through whose eyes we perceive it is this time not the suicidal victim, but her sometime lover André. Upon this "eternal spectator," himself an unfulfilled and disillusioned individual ("moths get into so many things, also into dreams," he remarks at the start of the play), is thrust the role of a visionary Orpheus who must coax Tordis back from the arms of death. By dint of the sheer force of his will and his desperate thoughts, he reaches out through space and time to save her, and to dispel forever the curse of the forlorn Villa Gullcry. (One critic has seen the entire play as a deliberate rejoinder to the black pessimism of a play like Anouilh's *Eurydice,* with its unmitigated insistence on man's aloneness and on the impossibility of ever escaping the past and beginning over again. [40])

The "realistic" framework within which the expressionistic dream play evolves is set in the atmospheric Café Bern, a theater café filled with red velvet sofas and memories, held "in the charming style of the eighties, painted on gauze transparencies which can in part disappear, in part be lit through to reveal entirely new vistas, entirely new effects." As the curtain rises, André has come here to the old café, after a prolonged absence, to fetch a letter which he has been told is waiting for him, and which proves to be from Tordis on her bleak island. Within this realm of the play, André's world, he functions as a voluble narrator, comfortably seated in his sofa. Recognizing the handwriting on the envelope, he launches at once into a long monologue of reminiscence, reliving, in somewhat sentimentalized terms, his youthful love affair with Tordis, the affluent daughter of an overly punctilious government bureaucrat behind whose back she "was engaged first to one, then to the next, and on around the table" (9). For a week they were lovers, met each day at the Café Bern; soon she moved on to the next, restlessly fleeing life's demands. André, who even at the age of eighteen seemed more at home in the closed, regimented world of Tordis's martinet father than he cares to admit, has since found sanctuary in the "tranquility" of his idealized wife-mother Marianne.

His repose is soon shattered, however, by the unexpected contents of the envelope in his hand: "an old photograph of an old woman in an old-fashioned hunting dress. At her feet lies a dog. A dog! *(Looks up quickly.)* The blue pekinese! *(Looks again at the photograph.)* Isabella de Creuith. That's it, that's her. The government official's aunt [actually his great-aunt]. Her brother built the house in his day, the lonely house on the cape by the lighthouse" (12–13). To unravel the meaning of the cryptic message, André's memory carries him back to a summer day on Iselø some months before. As the narrative of past events continues unbroken, the apparition of Tordis's world which the faded photograph conjures up in his mind presses in upon the reality of Café Bern. Within its confines, the contours of the desolate Villa Gullcry ("an immense pile with dragon heads and saga carvings, not a house but a living being") gradually materialize before our eyes. The continual, fluid interplay in the stage picture between André's café environment and the suggestive surrealistic elements of Iselø's unearthly dreamscape that impinge on it becomes in itself a large-scale visual metaphor for the thematic tension between vision and reality in the play. Erik Nordgreen's expressive designs for the original production ably realized this difficult technical process on the stage.

The initial phase of André's waking dream of Iselø is entirely recollective—an expository flashback to his coincidental encounter with Tordis last summer, when he and Marianne had visited the island. Tordis, galloping recklessly through the sand, had seemed to them "a female centaur," an aloof and discordant being whose adopted masculine traits served to shield her from emotional contact ("I have never known tenderness, never shown tenderness," she later admits). Her loveless and childless marriage—a union confined to the mainland, from which her trips to the island provide an escape—satisfies both social convention and her own unexpressed desire for revenge on her father: "My husband is the son I gave to

Father as recompense for the fact that I myself was a girl. No, he never reproached me, but it was always in the air. I very soon realized that the whole idea of woman was something inferior" (15). Such a revelation elicits no direct response, however, for even the consolation of dialogue, as a means of overcoming isolation, is denied to us and to Abell's characters.[41] The entire play is a dramatic image of aloneness and anomie, and the playwright has boldly restructured his form to mirror that concern, virtually abandoning the sequential give-and-take of conventional dialogue. In the early scenes André, apparently incapable of hearing the plea for help and compassion that lies close beneath the surface of Tordis's desperate chatter, is significantly limited to apathetic, third-person comments:

TORDIS. André, I can see what you're thinking. At some point we must give up part of our freedom, part of ourselves. I've done that, André. Done it gladly. But Iselø, Villa Gullcry, no one can take that from me. Here my freedom lives its own life. Here I own something I cannot see. Something invisible, something intangible—something—
ANDRÉ. She let her hands drop.
TORDIS. How shall I say it?
ANDRÉ. For a moment she sat, a bit disheartened, staring straight ahead. Then she turned quickly to Marianne.
TORDIS. Why not stay here, both of you. Stay a couple of days. Give me that pleasure. Sometimes one can—
ANDRÉ. Suddenly she stopped. It was as though she had caught sight of someone or something that made a cloud pass before the sun—but only for a moment.
TORDIS. Sometimes one can feel so terribly in need of friends. . . .

(18–19)

As even this brief sample indicates, *The Blue Pekinese* is a drama in which ordinary dialogue is rendered powerless. In its stead, the playwright has substituted an associational pattern of monologues, pauses, and silences to project his poetic image of human isolation. Silence is particularly important in this play, in which three of the eleven characters have no lines whatsoever. Olsen, the impassive café waiter, is a mute representative of the "real" world, on whom André's mental turmoil makes no visible impression. The complacent and maternal Marianne—in every sense the antithesis to the self-dispossessed Tordis (André calls them "two worlds separated by an invisible glass wall")—also remains silent. Like Olsen, Marianne

too belongs to a "safe" social reality which feels no compulsion to
interpret existence: "She is, she exists, her repose is my world," her
husband declares (92). Yet a third mute presence in the play is
Hansson, the lighthouse keeper's young assistant whose "uniform-
like blue" figure had cast the ominous shadow mentioned in the
above excerpt. Hansson *needs* no speech because (like Holofernes)
he is seen as the embodiment of an abstraction—in this case the
threat and the power of sheer physical masculinity. His is a force
feared by Tordis, and incorporated into the stage picture in the form
of Villa Gullcry's ponderously denotative "figurehead"—the peeling
statue of a merman "with storm-whipped cape and raised trident"
(13). The unadorned virility of the taciturn Hansson has not only
brought the lighthouse keeper's wife to bed with child, and be-
witched her impressionable sister Emily; it has also touched and
soiled the reserved Tordis, who attempts to escape from its tawdry
demands by escaping from life.

In addition to these silent characters, the landscape of *The Blue
Pekinese* is dotted with peripheral figures who are discussed at
length but who never appear—Tordis's husband, the members of
her oppressive family (all too familiar, perhaps, from Abell's earlier
plays), the cuckolded lighthouse keeper and his pregnant wife
(whose situation is used specifically as a grotesque reflection of Tordis's own). This "maze of details, parents and past" forming Tordis's
background requires an expository treatment which occupies nearly
one-third of the drama's duration, and which seems at times better
adapted to a novel than to a play. As André's dramatized recollection
of his fateful summer visit to Iselø continues, the venerable device
of an elderly local doctor—faithful family friend, plot mover, and
garrulous expositor—is employed to provide us with a rather full
narrative commentary on Tordis's antecedents, punctuated by scat-
tered third-person comments by André ("I shook my head" or "the
doctor looked for a long while at his cigar ash").

Chief among Tordis's forbears is her father's eccentric great-aunt
Isabella de Creuith, a redoubtable figure whose restless ghost still
roams Iselø, ceaselessly whistling for her playful and bell-collared
companion Dicky, the blue pekinese. ("She said it was blue.
Though, to be perfectly honest, it was hard for me to see. To my
eyes it seemed more grayish-brown. But nothing availed. She toler-
ated no contradictions. Dicky was blue!" explains the worthy physi-
cian (25)—though he hastily admits that his own "sense of the

supernatural can at best be characterized as underdeveloped.") Although she died when Tordis was six, Isabella belongs to a timeless past which is very much alive in the play, and which coalesces with present and future in its fluid time scheme. (Her "slightly prehistoric, somewhat masculine hunting dress" is said to stem from "the year Sadi Carnot was murdered"—an event which in fact took place in 1832!) From the aristocratic Isabella, Tordis has inherited not only her crumbling island house but also the old woman's unhappy fate—to live immured in an egoistic and costly loneliness "that keeps all things at a distance." Though she spoke to her only once as a small girl, Tordis recalls, "every time she saw me, she gave a cheerful blast on her whistle, touched her cap in a greeting, and disappeared over the heath with Dicky at her heels" (33). Twelve years after Isabella's death, Tordis returned to Iselø to take up her inheritance—and the burden of the past which it entailed:

TORDIS.   . . . The day I came of age, I journeyed up here. I arrived alone at dusk, and came out here at once—out on the terrace. You may laugh if you like, I don't mind, but the first thing I heard out on the heath was a welcoming whistle.
DOCTOR.   The nights up here are filled with sounds.
TORDIS.   The wind in the heather sounded like distant bells. And in a spot above the heath, the sky became blue.
ANDRÉ.   The blue pekinese? What do you mean? Was it really blue?
TORDIS.   Yes, as blue as the sky.
ANDRÉ.   As the sky?
TORDIS.   I think so.
ANDRÉ.   Think so?
DOCTOR.   Yes, our blue friend Dicky departed for the eternal hunting ground many years before Tordis was born.
ANDRÉ.   Before Tordis was born? But didn't she say just a moment ago—?

(34–35)

André's bewildered question goes unanswered. Involuntarily, he too becomes caught up in the mystical atmosphere of "this night peopled with specters, specters of the dead, specters of the unborn": "In a spot above the heath, the sky had become blue. It was as if a world, an alien world was born of that word, that one word—blue. It hovered in the air like a hazy globe, a playful pearl in the hands of heaven. If I were a poet—(*stops suddenly*). Without realizing it, I must have said it aloud" (36). His unthinking remark acquires unexpected potency. Tordis, sensing evasion as well as inspiration behind the ambiguous phrase, tells André ("almost aggressively") that, when she is dead, he is to have the only existing photograph of Aunt Isabella and Dicky. This dark promise ends the long memory sequence, and André, still seated at his café table, abruptly grasps the intent behind the faded picture in his hands, inscribed in Tordis's own writing with the words, "If I were a poet": "The letter is a cry, a terrified cry for help, why else would she send it? No, no, she doesn't want help, she sent it here, here it might have lain for days, for weeks . . ." (39). His decision, activated by his recollection of Iselø, to reach out and draw Tordis back from her carefully premeditated suicide is a major turning point in the play, introducing a new movement and a swifter, less pensive rhythm. He is compelled to recognize and combat not only Tordis's lonely decision to die, but also his own moral complicity in that decision—the selfishness and ultimate bankruptcy of his comfortably conditional "if":

Therein lies the flight, the flight from a shared responsibility toward one another. You perceive in a glimpse the invisible circle. Others, yourself. Feel in your hands the urge to reach out, but as you do reach out you look back, see the chair where you have sat so safely, so safely as a spectator. Where is there a parachute? That single word "if." (92)

When his efforts to reach Iselø by telephone are frustrated by a fierce November storm and by the maddening interruptions of an empty-headed café guest, André overcomes both distance and time by the sheer force of empathetic imagination. It is not his frantic telephone call but his intense telepathic vision of Tordis' hurricane-lashed island which summons her before him, already shrouded in Isabella de Creuith's black and blood-red shawl and prepared to follow the old woman into eternity.

Isolated at the very center of the play is the important and revealing scene in which Tordis and André talk, for the first time in the drama, *to* one another (to the extent that Abell's characters are ever able to do so). Having carried her isolation to its logical destructive extreme, even Tordis feels the need of having "one single witness" to her desperate act:

TORDIS.   No, André, no—you must not laugh—
ANDRÉ.   Laugh—!

TORDIS. —or think I'm taking myself too seriously. But in the midst of a helplessness one can feel the need to—unburden oneself. Except that one can't, one hasn't the ability. Last summer you said—that evening on the terrace—if I were a poet.

ANDRÉ. I didn't hear my own voice until I had said it. I was miles away.

TORDIS. The chasm—never had I seen it so clearly before.

ANDRÉ. The chasm—?

TORDIS. Between you and me. Between me and both of you. You rested on a corner of Marianne's repose. Marianne, about whom clusters of children can crawl without disrupting her repose for a second. . . . From your world of tranquility around Marianne, Marianne's world, you regarded me with wide, surprised child's eyes as a strange woman, of whom one is in reality a little afraid. A strange woman. Stranger to everyone. That was your judgment.

ANDRÉ. I didn't judge you, I have never judged you.

TORDIS. Without realizing it. Yes, that night. Your judgment was a shrug of the shoulders. . . .

(62–64)

She has accepted his judgment, Tordis tells him, and she urges him to "forget me, forget me as I forgot the world around me." At this critical moment, however, another "character" unexpectedly intervenes, as the sound of bells and a summer-blue sky in the midst of an autumn storm announce the magical presence of the invisible Dicky. The blue pekinese (like Larsen's melody in Abell's very first play) is a broad-spectrumed metaphor for the manifold demands and potentialities of life, the energy and truth of existence. Significantly, André too has now become capable of actually seeing the remarkable beast:

ANDRÉ. It must be difficult to move about with such a long-haired coat, in the heather especially.

TORDIS. Not for Dicky. *(The sky has slowly changed color, the sound of bells comes nearer and nearer.)* Come, Dicky—come on.

ANDRÉ. It's much bigger than I had ever imagined, even bigger than the Scottish sheep-dogs. [42]

TORDIS. And then that color, that color—*(The sound of bells has now come very near, the stage is filled with clear silver bells.)* No, Dicky, Dicky—*(André makes a defensive gesture.)* You mustn't jump up, do you hear, Dicky? The strange man doesn't like that one bit. Sit, sit. . . .

(65–66)

The intrusion of the sprightly Dicky at this particular point is propitious. Although the confrontation between André and Tordis reaches no immediate resolution and she remains, as the first-act curtain falls, undecided whether to follow him back into life or to accompany Aunt Isabella into nothingness, the salutary presence of the symbolic pekinese clearly foretells the play's affirmative outcome.

The much shorter second act forms the final movement of this surrealistic fantasia, played against the background of the storm and the phrases of the haunting waltz (composed by Niels Viggo Bentzon) to which Isabella de Creuith "dances away the shadows" of Iselø—"the waltz which will conclude my last ball. My last, my last" (73). In this final section of the play, fantasy has displaced reality entirely. André—although still followed about by his red velvet sofa from Café Bern—is the spectator-dreamer no longer; he has now crossed completely over into the vision, and is fully involved in it as an active participant.

Side by side with the Doctor's gradual discovery of Tordis' covertly administered overdose of sleeping pills (that is, the "realistic" motivation for her last-minute recovery) runs another, more crucial line of psychological action. At its core is the struggle of wills between André and Isabella de Creuith which, in the end, proves far more decisive for Tordis' rescue than any medical diagnosis. André's splendidly declamatory attack on Isabella ("an egoistic old maid who in a twilight whim pointed round the horizon and said to a six-year-old girl: all this is yours, you are my heir, my heir to everything. Everything. Your life, your destiny, your defeat") is scathing:

Eternity's neighbor you imagined yourself to be. I know what that means. I have felt the urge myself. All of us feel it, we have it in our blood, all we refugees from a petty world with its flattened-out rules that threaten to rob our personal touch of its fragrance. In terror we move away, move up into higher spheres, the lonely spheres. . . . We who have only one belief, one religion, one conviction—ourselves. (88)

Behind "such strong words," however, the old woman recognizes clearly the self-deceiver, "the forgetful individual who, in order to conceal what he has forgotten, sets himself the highest goals, so high, so high, so perfect in their beauty that they can never be attained. The fact that one has them is enough" (93). Quietly she lays bare the self-pity and self-delusion of this moral escape-artist, who loses himself in humanitarian rhetoric and his superficial involvement with "others" (*andre* in Danish) and who finds security in

his (conveniently tongue-tied!) idealization of Marianne. Their encounter brings André to recognize his own betrayal of Tordis—in
reality a repetition of *his* betrayal of *her* in their youth: "I left her
facing the darkness in that isolation which she pretended to love. A
pretence she hoped would evoke my opposition. A hope, a plea that
she would be contradicted. But I failed to take up the challenge"
(91).

Isabella, determined to use this night on Iselø to end forever her
own restless dance on earth, is the strongest figure in this final
movement of the play; she, not André, holds the key to its resolution. Tordis' salvation will expiate the crime she has come to
regret—the thoughtless, vengeful act of willing upon a girl of six a
crushing fate, which struck down the very one she "last of all wished
to strike" (109). Isabella's trump card in this metaphysical game of
life and death is Esmond, the lighthouse keeper's yet unborn son,
whose pale specter she and Dicky have pursued throughout the
stormy November night. On this very night, the lighthouse keeper's
wife is to give birth, but Esmond, the child whose name and whole
future have been decided beforehand by his mother and the pathet-
ic Emily, refuses to be born into this shabby world of dreams and
despair. "Always these dreams. You're knee deep in dreams. Even
before a guy is born, he has to put up with living in other people's
dreams, and no sooner does he come into the world before he's
made to continue the dream that his parents couldn't get to come
true themselves," he declares in his curiously awkward jargon (104).
The complaint echoes one of the prevailing themes of Abell's early
comedies.

Once more, however, Dicky's indispensable presence bodes well
for the outcome. The unborn Esmond, depicted in the play as an
ungainly, robust young boy, is at first confused and frightened by
the dog's deceptively "fear-inspiring countenance," but he overcomes his initial timidity and plays happily with the delighted
pekinese. In Esmond's eager but uncertain hands the playwright
has placed the central choice between life and death. Life in all its
biological crudity is no joke, personified as it is in the gross (and
rather melodramatically conceived) figure of the Midwife from
Vrem, whose sinister shadow is, Isabella reminds us portentously,
the darkness "through which we must pass before the dance is
done." The screams and protests of her unborn charges are
answered by the obscene truth of her hoarse and cynical song:

I am the midwife from Vrem. Come to me, little ones, little newly-boiled shrimp in a pool of slimy blood. A smack on the backside, and I grant you breath. . . . And then we meet again, when I prepare you and lay you in boxes—in boxes, in boxes. . . . Three shovels on the lid—bum-daderabum—then down in the earth, slimy and wormy. . . . (100)

Ironically, Tordis is the character who implores Esmond to forget the midwife's "song from hell" and to accept the gift of life gratefully—but it proves to be the challenge of André's skepticism ("when it comes right down to it, you haven't really got the will to live") which provokes the "divine urge to contradict" in the truculent youngster:

Will? Will to live? And what about you? And her? And her? Dammit, you look like three shipwrecked people on a raft. . . . I've got plenty of will. The blown-down tent you've left behind you, that goddam well (pardon my swearing) needs to be raised up again by fresh hands. . . . We're put here to live, make ourselves worthy to live—live, be part of life! (105)

"No power on earth" can hold him back from embracing life "unconditionally," he now tells them fiercely, and his headstrong, last-minute change of attitude becomes the force needed to exorcize Tordis' own despair and restore her will to begin life once more.

Esmond's forthright demeanor, his colorful jargon, and even his paternity (the popular Hansson) all qualify him for the role of the common man upon whose innate soundness and vitality so many of Abell's plays have depended for their resolution. Nevertheless, it would be a fundamental oversimplification to interpret Esmond's deliberately adolescent and impulsively optimistic espousal of "the will to live" as the idealistic "message" which the playwright wishes to proclaim. Particularly the play's first reviewers were generally satisfied that it depicted simply "the conversion of a shallow upperclass woman to—we must be content to say life, since its direction or result is not indicated."[43] Abell's dream play is, however, no naively affirmative paean to "life"; it is a complex, musically structured allegory on the human condition, in which life—for better or for worse—reaffirms itself, "unconditionally."[44] The drama's conclusion, played against the background of the luminous, pekinese-blue sky of Iselø, is basically open-ended: Isabella de Creuith is free at last to take her leave; Tordis and Esmond go off, in different directions, toward their new goals; the scenic elements of Café Bern glide once more into place, and André is reunited with Marianne as the final curtain falls. Upon what may lie beyond the moment of existential choice, the playwright does not speculate.

Although simple in its fundamental situation, *The Blue Pekinese* is far from unambiguous. Moreover, both its unusual narrative style and the scope and beauty of its carefully instrumented theatrical images add greatly to the difficulty of performing it effectively. At its core, this work, like *Three from Minikoi,* deals with the intrinsically ambivalent conflict between faith and doubt. Between these complementary opposites we vacillate, Abell argues, at one moment wishing for the will to believe, at the next instant "resting our heads on the doubt through which we find a balance." The doubleness which Abell finds inherent in this conflict and which deepens the complexity of his vision in the range of plays from *Days on a Cloud* to *The Blue Pekinese* is succinctly summarized in the closing words of *Minikoi,* as the poet looks for the last time on the new world of the East: "Come back, my doubt, and grant me again that faith without which we cannot live."

CHAPTER 5

Last Plays

I *Anderseniana*

IN the dramatization of history, Strindberg declares in the fifth of
his famous *Open Letters to the Intimate Theater*, "the purely
human is of major interest, and history the background; the inner
struggles of souls awaken more sympathy than the combat of sol-
diers or the storming of walls." In his own cycle of history plays—
each one structured to focus on an intense moment of human
crises—he therefore "made the major characters live by taking
blood and nerves out of [his] own life" and by "avoiding the undramatic form of the chronicle or the narrative."[1] Although the
spirit of this shrewd advice might seem, at first glance, to have
animated Kjeld Abell's historical festival play, *Andersen eller Hans
Livs Eventyr (Andersen, or the Fairytale of His Life)*, it is precisely
in Strindberg's terms that this often overlooked work falls short.
Commissioned by the Royal Theater to celebrate the sesquicenten-
nial of Hans Christian Andersen's birth and first produced on April
3, 1955, Abell's elaborate homage is a mélange of chronicle,
pageantry, and narrative snippets culled from Andersen's autobiography (*Mit Livs Eventyr* [*The Fairytale of My Life*]) and his tales.
The result is a clever enough scissors-and-paste job that fails, however, to achieve either the compositional logic or the dramatic con-
sistency of a comparable commemorative piece like the charming
Lot No. 267 East District. The stupendous "mechanical and electri-
cal magic" of John Price's production created, most critics felt,
"truly a splendid piece of Anderseniana"—a pyrotechnic display
possessing "talented technique, brilliant visual impressions, but no
visions" and ultimately lacking "that profound grasp of the subject's
simple humanity" which alone could have brought Andersen himself to life.[2] That Abell, at the height of his powers, should have
fallen short of doing so appears doubly surprising in view of the

abiding influence which Andersen's style and tone have had on his writing.

From the very start of his career, in almost every review of *The Melody that Got Lost*, resonances of Andersen were noticed and singled out. Questioned by an interviewer about such a comparison, the young playwright pronounced himself "in utter despair over the idea, I can have nothing whatsoever to do with it; I take it as a spontaneous result of the play's fundamentally Danish mentality, and I suppose that those who expressed the idea were unable in their haste to think of anything else to write except H. C. Andersen, who was undeniably Danish to his fingertips, and so it just popped into their pens."[3] In an article written by him five years later, however, a more mature Abell declared that, reading Andersen's works, "one had the strangest sensation of being turned into a piano which is being played upon. You discover that, just like the piano, you are filled with tones—pictures and impressions and sensations—that are waiting and longing to be called forth and combined in a totally new manner."[4] In fact, it is perhaps no exaggeration to say that no Scandinavian dramatist—with the possible exception of Strindberg—derived greater inspiration from Andersen's unusual poetic insight and genius.

The nature of that inspiration is a subject of its own, to which only the briefest allusion can be made here. Linguistic craftsmanship is naturally a consideration of utmost importance: both Abell's unorthodox and commanding treatment of grammatical construction, and his adoption of a writing style that corresponds so closely to the rhythm, structure, and usage of spoken language are traits which obviously relate his work to Andersen's innovative achievements as a prose stylist.[5] Moreover, Abell's highly personalized travel descriptions are often worthy counterparts to Andersen's own unsurpassed word-pictures of Sweden (*I Sverrig* [*In Sweden*]), Spain (*I Spanien* [*In Spain*]), Greece and Turkey (*En Digters Bazar* [*A Poet's Bazaar*]). Striking, too, is their shared tendency to recognize an invisible bond between things and people, and hence to endow inanimate objects with life and speech ("Persons can, even when they speak, remain silent," we are reminded in *Minikoi*, "but things, which are doomed to eternal silence, never cease their stream of talk"). Finally and not least important, Abell's own *eventyr* ("fairy tale" hardly covers the ground, either for him or for his great model) further reinforce the sense of an affinity between these two

writers. His fable of the dreary and disconsolate Anna and the marble dove ("Marmorduen" ["The Marble Dove"], 1935), his tale of
Adam and Eve's first night outside Paradise ("Den første aften"
["The First Evening"], 1941), and his stories of Saint Peter's visit to
earth on a pitch-dark night during the German occupation ("Myrer
og modsigelseslyst" ["Ants and Contrariness"], 1940) and of the
sensitive and talkative taxi that recalls those years ("Den følsomme
taxa" ["The Sensitive Taxi"], 1946) are all telling examples of his
absorption in the ironic, essentially oral art of the storyteller.[6] Most
of his tales were also first read in public by the author himself.

The artistic bond between Kjeld Abell and H. C. Andersen is thus
strong and tangible. Perhaps the very realization of this affinity
tended to exacerbate critical disappointment in the "gigantic
souvenir shop" which *Andersen, or the Fairytale of His Life*
became—"an unreasonably extensive exhibition of Anderseniana,"
Harald Engberg found it, in which the basic idea "drowns in shouts
of hurrah, while the image of the poet congeals into a silhouette in
the most banal of apotheoses."[7] The idea to which this critic refers is
a promising but undeveloped conceit, centering on the wistful
figure of the old Woman in the Yellow Satin Coat—an incomplete
Andersen character whose final macabre journey to the grave is
sketched in a single episode of his fascinating prose collection *Bil-
ledbog uden Billeder (Picture Book without Pictures)*. "No one
knows me. I am only half a story, without a heading, without a title,
just 'The Tenth Evening,' a conclusion to something that doesn't
belong anywhere," she declares in Abell's play.[8] Although the full
complement of Andersen's fairy-tale characters is summoned to
Odense for the great torchlight celebration honoring him, the unhappy Woman in Yellow Satin receives no invitation. In the chival-
rous company of the Man in the Moon, who of course first told her
story to the struggling young poet in his garret, she therefore em-
barks on a dizzying odyssey through the teeming universe of her
creator's fantasy in search of her true place in it. Finally, from the
lips of the poet himself, this unfinished character receives her answer:

WOMAN.   My complete story! Poet, write me over again. Male characters
   long for power and we—I have never before said we—we long for love.
ANDERSEN.   Love—Yes, Woman in your Yellow Satin Coat, your half
   story is written in the little mermaid, in little Ida who never grows up, in
   many others, you are to be found everywhere.

WOMAN.   Then may the larks laugh, may they laugh and sing their song.
   Oh, poet, poet, to the town-hall festival—for now I am invited.

(84)

And, true to the spirit of the occasion, they dance off together to join the festival of lights which concludes the play. Clara Pontoppidan's finely etched, ironic old maid in yellow and Holger Gabrielsen's sparkling, top-hatted Man in the Moon were able to transform this witty but only partially realized literary footnote into a workable framework for the production, but their art could not save the main figure in the drama from suffering the old woman's fate—to remain a botched, inconclusive character.

   The play—virtually a ballet-drama in which intricate choreography plays an essential role—is structured as a series of contrasting moments, and it juxtaposes excerpts from Andersen's writing with effective visual impressions. Probably the most vivid of these moments in the original production was the largely pantomimic sequence in which the awkward young Hans Christian, using his broad hat as a tambourine, dances his renowned gavotte for the influential ballerina Anna Schall. Crushed beneath the weight of the derisive laughter that echoes from the darkness beyond the stage, he falls on his knees in prayer—and rises to discover beside him those magical but highly problematic boots of fortune, called *Lykkens Galocher*. Borrowing from the tale of that name, Abell introduces its two symbolic personages as Andersen's inseparable companions throughout his life's journey: "The one was perhaps not Fortune herself but one of her handmaidens' handmaidens, who distributes Fortune's lesser rewards; the other, looking so profoundly serious, is Sorrow, her errands are always run by her own exalted self so she can be sure that they are carried out properly" (22). But, remarked the review in *Politiken*, "after a few minutes of life [these deities] stiffen into Thorvaldsen-like decorations attractively flanking the proscenium opening." In a manner which does in fact recall his early festival ballet "Thorvaldsen," Abell elects to delineate the object of his homage mainly in terms of anthropomorphized renderings of his creations—while the artist himself becomes little more than a marble bust (or in this case a silhouette) to be laurel-crowned in the prescribed fashion.

   The character of Andersen himself is introduced relatively late in the play, and the kaleidoscopic "fairy tale of his life" is condensed into one central episode drawn from his early career—his first momentous visit to Rome during the autumn and winter of 1833. Here, against the atmospheric background of Niels Bjørn Larsen's picturesquely choreographed Roman carnival and Svend Johansen's monumental reconstruction of the Scala di Spagna , the melancholy young poet, preoccupied with the fate of his newly finished dramatic poem *Agnete and the Merman,* is seen waiting in despair for an encouraging letter from home ("What a night have I not suffered. I had fever in my blood. How close was I not to ending this miserable life!" [53]). Predictably, when a letter finally does arrive—from Andersen's loyal but cruelly undiplomatic friend Edvard Collin—it not only castigates *Agnete* but also brings him word of his mother's death.[9] The actual text of this often-reprinted epistle (slightly edited to cast Collin in the worst possible light) is delivered in a long narrative reminiscent of André's monologues in *The Blue Pekinese.* Only the pleas and encouragement of his characters save the sensitive poet from its shatteringly demoralizing effect. Hence, this (historically rather contrived) moment of crisis is potentially comparable to similar situations in Abell's earlier fantasias on the theme of self-destruction. However, the full dramatic impact of Andersen's personal crisis remains unarticulated in this play, and its resolution is disappointingly schematic, resting on a repetition of overworked clichés wrung from the pages of *The Ugly Duckling.* Inevitably, Ebbe Rode's physically lifelike rendering of the character seemed to reviewers of the first production "splendid in his expressions of emerging conceit, touching in his fondness for esthetic pleasure, but alas, without that intellect from which the visions sprang, without that luminosity on his brow that foretells blessedness." "In short," Harald Engberg concluded, "Andersen well copied, but without genius." "The festival dramatist has respectfully avoided the simple intensity of the poet's own personality," added *Berlingske Tidende,* "and gives us instead an entertaining fairy tale about the overwhelming capability of the modern stage."

This montage of theatrical contrasts and surprises reaches a visual highpoint in the whirling, dancing carnival of fairy-tale characters that follows the reading of Collin's gloomy letter. This fantastic carnival is in turn juxtaposed with the play's most unexpected sequence—a long, dramatized reading of *Skarnbassen (The Dung-Beetle),* Andersen's exquisite fairy-tale paraphrase of the Arabic proverb once suggested to him by Dickens: "When they came to shoe the Pasha's horses, the beetle stretched out his leg." The tale is introduced into Abell's play as a wry comment by the poet on the

Woman in Yellow Satin's romantic dream of her "prince in shining black"—but the importunate figure of the self-important and peevish black beetle (made up in performance as a demonic caricature of its creator) is clearly also meant to project a grotesquely distorted reflection of Andersen's own self:

THE SMITH.   But why was the horse given golden shoes? Don't you understand that?
THE DUNG-BEETLE.   Understand? I understand that it shows contempt for me, it's an outrage—and so now I shall go out into the wide world.
SMITH.   Buzz off!
THE DUNG-BEETLE.   Ruffian!
ANDERSEN.   Said the dung-beetle, and then it went outside, flew a short distance, and now it was in a lovely little flower garden. . . .

(74)

The playwright's use of the style and tone of "story theater" is skilful. Although some critics have disagreed with his choice of this tale, the fable of the ambitious dung-beetle's picaresque journey, its soliloquy on the injustices of this world ("Now I know the world! It is a base world! I am the only honorable individual in it!"), and the final epiphany when, alighting at last in the mane of the imperial horse, it "realizes" that the noble animal's golden shoes have surely been put there for *its* sake form a splendidly absurd countermotif that balances the fanfares of the main story. Nevertheless, this theme—like the Pirandellian motif of the Woman in Yellow Satin who searches for an explanation of the half-life the author has given her—is only tentatively and incompletely developed. It is conclusively obliterated in the concluding *fortissimo* of the poet's laurel-crowning.

Surely the most cutting satirical barb concealed in Abell's eclectic homage is lodged in the Man in the Moon's fearsome vision of the universe of endlessly proliferating tourist souvenirs that will come to constitute the ultimate testimony to Andersen's fame:

The Little Mermaid in a thousand versions, in all sizes, all shapes, on ashtrays, on vases and pitchers, plates and platters, millions of platters in the finest, finest blue of the Sound. Continue with swans, go right through the catalogue, the whole collected deluxe edition, there is not a thing which cannot be used, on scarves, on knickknacks, and on lampshades . . . and when all has been used, then start on the poet, his silhouette, his profile, his umbrella, his boots, nothing shall be allowed to escape its destiny. . . . (70–71)

However, *Politiken* remarked, "as the evening unfolded in the length and breadth of its details, this *bon mot* became a boomerang that turned back against the production itself." The depiction of "the purely personal element" which Strindberg regarded as so important in this genre—in this case a sense of the pain and the greatness of Andersen himself—was subordinated to the spectacle of an elaborate mechanical toyshop filled with life-size souvenirs. "Elevator traps go down, backdrops fly aloft, surprises happen—there is hardly *one* quiet moment," wrote yet another reviewer, whose opinion that "Kjeld Abell sometimes exploits theatrical resources almost *too* cleverly"[10] sums up the critical consensus toward *Andersen, or the Fairytale of His Life*. Its legendary Royal Theater production, seen for a total of thirty-two performances, was a theatrical experience of unparalleled magnificence (though the anecdote that one entire performance had to be cancelled when a lighting man became ill tells its own story!). The play itself, however, seems in retrospect a work of relatively minor importance in Abell's production, of interest chiefly as a proclamation of its author's unmistakable affinity for, and indebtedness to, the subject of his biographical festival.

II   The Lady of the Camelias (1959)

"Why *Camille?*" demanded Brooks Atkinson when this popular potboiler was revived on Broadway in 1956: "it is inconceivable that anyone should have an artistic interest in the old Dumas *fils* rumpus."[11] Substantially the same question must also have occurred to many of Kjeld Abell's critics before his long, three-act drama *Kameliadamen (The Lady of the Camelias)* opened at the New Theater in Copenhagen on March 17, 1959. However, even the slightest acquaintance with Abell's many previous re-explorations of fictional or historical situations and (predominantly female) characters—Eve, Dyveke, Judith, Maria Vetsera, and so on—ought to prepare one for the fact that his approach to the threadbare tale of the consumptive courtesan would inevitably be an unconventional one. His *Kameliadame* is based not on the famous play but on the lesser-known Dumas novel from which it was quarried, also entitled *La dame aux camélias* and written in 1847. In his modern reinterpretation, Abell's boldest stroke is the introduction of the original author, Alexandre Dumas, as the narrator of the story as well as a major participant in it. The result is an unusual and fascinating experiment which, although at times verbose and even exasperating in performance, succeeds in placing its shopworn subject matter in an entirely new dramatic perspective.

The romantic, ill-fated affair between Armand Duval and Marguerite Gautier, over which countless generations of audiences have wept, is here desentimentalized and utilized by the playwright as a basic pattern which gives shape to a far more intricate dramatic fabric, woven together of intersecting and interdependent lines of thematic development. Nevertheless, although Marguerite and Armand are viewed in a new light and given new dialogue to speak, the familiar chain of events in their eternal relationship is (wisely) retained to form the core of Abell's version. "Marguerite's big scenes, from meeting through happiness to ridicule and death, are all here, formed in a language which . . . can certainly be listened to (something which the old play certainly cannot) today," declared one of the production's most enthusiastic reviewers.[12] Thus, once again the most beautiful and envied prostitute in all of Paris encounters the abashed young Armand outside her box at the premiere of *Bérenice,* and once again her mercantile heart is touched for the first time by love when they speak together at her dazzling evening party. Their enchanted summer of bliss in the idyllic pastoral surroundings of Bougival is projected in an effective scene which provided Abell's star, Bodil Kjer, with one of the emotional highpoints in her vibrant performance. "The vision of this tenderly loving courtesan in her Garden of Eden has," remarked Harald Engberg, "for a brief moment made [the playwright] what he otherwise never was—an erotic writer—and it has given him the power to achieve what even erotic writers find difficult—the depiction of happiness, the physical-spiritual miracle between two people, their awakening in Paradise. . . . "[13]

Although Marguerite is pursued to Bougival by her past life, in the guise of the procuress Prudence and the voluptuous Olympe (for "once a member of the sisterhood, always a member, no one can escape"[14]), it is Armand's father who functions as the heartless Forza del Destino in this bourgeois drama. As the carefree summer fades into September, his arrival drives the happy lovers from their Eden forever. In Abell's reshaping of this tear-soaked scene, Old Duval is cleansed of the implacability of Dumas' tyrannical and choleric father figure. He is at first reluctant to speak his mind, and Marguerite is compelled to voice the ruthless demands she sees written in his sympathetic face. The end result is, however, the same. Duval's pleading is skilful, embodying that insidious social and moral conventionality which, in Abell's view, represents the denial and destruction of life itself: "If you love him as I believe you do, you would overcome the selfishness in your love and release him from this prison, before slow torture robs his love of its life. You gave him a gift, the greatest of all—take that from him and he will retain it, try to retain it together and both will lose it" (85). Whether or not she is actually convinced by these romantic clichés, Marguerite realizes that she has no alternative but to relinquish Armand. Facing the sacrifice imposed on her, she writes to her absent lover that she is leaving Bougival to resume her former colorful existence. Dumas rang down his poignant third-act curtain on Armand's reading of the fateful letter's first few words—and Abell shrewdly closes his long second act on precisely the same climactic note.

By contrast, the final act of *Kameliadamen* swerves dangerously close to discursive anticlimax. ("By the time [Marguerite] reaches her death scene," wrote one of the play's harshest first-night critics, "everything around her had long since been talked to death by the author."[15]) Continuing to follow the progression of the original story, Armand, wounded by the apparent perfidy of his former mistress, seeks consolation in the simple but superabundant charms of Olympe—described by Dumas, the narrator, as "a sumptuous cornucopia of buttocks and breasts." However, the explosive Dumas *coup de théâtre* in which the angry young man vengefully denounces Marguerite before a ballroom-full of Olympe's astonished guests and then humiliates her publicly by flinging money at her feet is rather awkwardly defused by dramatizing the incident without the witnesses, thereby defeating the purpose of his outrageous gesture. For the misjudged and forsaken heroine, reduced to poverty and worn out by illness and grief, nothing remains but death—but she is given a good deal to say about the nature of her life and love before expiring: "Naked we come into this world, naked we depart from it. Everyone may believe that he buys a petal of the flower—but only Armand made it unfold with those petals which can never be bought" (107). No repentant and solicitous Armand returns at the last moment to console her in Abell's play, yet Marguerite dies convinced that his love "will never die. I believed then that I did the right thing, now I know that I did. Only by love can worlds be overturned" (108). Where Dumas ends, however, Abell begins. While the touching death of the courtesan resolves *La dame aux camélias,* this same event, framed in a much more complex and ambiguous thematic context, is in reality the point of departure for the poetic exploration of love and its power over death in *Kameliadamen.* At the heart of that exploration lies the irresolvable dilemma posed by the two conflicting questions to which Marguerite's fate gives rise: "What is it that we human beings do to one another?" cries Armand, wounded by her cruelty; "What is it that we human beings neglect to do, to do *for* one another?" demands Dumas, moved to compassion by her sorrow.

Abell's drama actually begins after Marguerite's death, and unfolds in the shadowy study of Alexandre Dumas. Here, the author is visited by his alter ego, Armand Duval, who comes to him in order "to find again and see again the face I love":

DUMAS.   One young man among thousands—and yet he had to be the one who, like an arcadian flute player, all unsuspecting had descended from lightheartedness and spring into the valley of the great whores.
ARMAND.   Forgive me—that I—
DUMAS.   The tension that had for several seconds held us locked in a vise loosened its grip.
ARMAND.   —that I call on you at this late hour.
DUMAS.   With a look as if to say: not at all—I bowed a welcome and waved a hand in the direction of the armchair, then walked to the fireplace, stood with an elbow resting on the mantelpiece. The staging was perfect. No one could see that in reality I was forced, just as he was, to struggle for composure.
ARMAND.   That I intrude into your life at all.
DUMAS.   He could hardly have realized the full implication of his words.

(21)

The intense symbiotic relationship between these two figures, the artist and his creation, constitutes a central motif in the play. The bond between them, reflected even in the identity of their initials, is of course suggested by the historical circumstances themselves. *La Dame aux camélias* found its inspiration in its young author's own brief and painful love affair with the illustrious courtesan Alphonsine Plessis, called Marie Duplessis, the model for Marguerite. Behind the rather banal romantic narrative by Dumas *fils,* Abell has sensed, and has embroidered upon, the writer's genuine emotional involvement in the subject. Hence, Abell's Armand is, as one critic proposes, "the author's twin brother, his alter ego, and at the same time his victim, the object of his insatiable, cold curiosity,"[16] but he is also the rival of Dumas, who has fallen "hopelessly in love with another's love"—that is, with his own heroine. "My feelings for him, were they friendly or the opposite?" the painfully introspective Dumas asks himself. "In the strangest sense there was an identity between us, but in reverse order—he was the one who had loved Marguerite, I the one who could have loved her" (24).

The Dumas of Abell's drama, like André in *The Blue Pekinese*, fancies himself to be "the skeptical spectator who keeps his own personality under detached observation." From his table at the sidewalk café outside Belle Préférence, "full of sober experience and imagined knowledge," he watches and charts the stream of life which passes. Yet somehow his imaginary creation has achieved an independent existence of its own, "as though at the crossroads between art and reality I had created, out of my own self, another, out of the doubt of my experience had created a belief in the miracle between human beings" (36). What was to be a "playful mental experiment" turns against him, and he finds himself drawn into it as an emotionally engaged participant. "My tale—his—this evening it begins to tell itself," he declares toward the very beginning of the play. In the darkness of his creator's workshop, Armand retells and relives the events of his relationship with Marguerite—always under the watchful scrutiny of his double, the poet posed at the mantelpiece: "The spiritual torments in which he lost himself gave me the opportunity to move on my own, to let my imagination experience all the small details he overlooked, while at the same time I followed his words like a faithful shadow" (39). Within the surrealistic scenes of the love affair which materialize in the darkened space by means of lighting effects, both the artist and his alter ego move freely—but Dumas' reflective comments emphasize again and again the gulf between them:

The greatest essential difference between him and me—suddenly I understood it. My actions drowned on the way in contemplation, in hesitation, in for and against, while he acted blindly, from a spontaneity which I must at one time have possessed but suppressed in order to be able to move freely out and in among other destinies instead. But always outside, outside—." (45–46)

Nowhere in the play is this "essential difference" more evident, perhaps, than in the implied contrast between their respective re-

sponses to Marguerite's death. Like his counterpart in life, Dumas
has returned to Paris after a long absence in time to attend the
auction sale of the courtesan's belongings. Here, almost surrepti-
tiously, he secures for himself the inscribed copy of Abbé Prevost's
romantic novel *Manon Lescaut* which Armand once dedicated to his
mistress, and which the young man comes to reclaim. Meanwhile,
Armand's reaction when he discovers that Marguerite has died represents a violent, impulsive antithesis to Dumas' cautious, esthetic
response—refusing to believe in her death, he opens her grave in
Monmartre Cemetery, and is compelled to look upon the decaying,
featureless corpse of his beloved. This grisly episode, described in
all its palpable horror, projects a vision which purges the lyrical
scenes of romance which follow of their residue of idealized sentimentality. "The reality of death is recognized and maintained, and
precisely for this reason life and love become for the first time a
miracle in earnest," Tage Hind has argued. "This painful realism" is
"the condition on which the concluding vision [Marguerite's death
scene] depends for its theatrically convincing realization."[17]

"The mystery of artistic creation is the same as that of birth,"
Pirandello declares in his famous preface to *Six Characters in Search
of an Author*. Once conceived, a character becomes "a living creature on a plane of life superior to the changeable existence of every
day."[18] Inevitably, Abell's preoccupation, both in *Andersen* and in
this play, with the complex metaphysical bond between the artist
and the characters of his art calls to mind Pirandello's influential
theories. "Born alive," Pirandello's six rejected characters returned
to him "in the solitude of his study" to plead their cause. "In this
struggle for existence that they have had to wage with me," he
continues, they gained independent life, becoming "characters that
can move and talk on their own initiative; already see themselves as
such; have learned to defend themselves against me." Comments
such as these seem to apply with almost equal validity to
Kameliadamen, in which, as one scholar argues, "the stage is in
reality the poet's mind, in this case the mind of Dumas."[19] His
characters acquire life, but their life is at the same time a reflection
of the inner processes of the poet—an expression, Pirandello would
say, "of the passion and torment which for so many years have been
the pangs of [his] spirit." Pirandello concludes his preface with a
well-known remark that Dumas himself might equally well have
appropriated: "The poet, unknown to them, as if looking on at a

distance throughout the whole period of the experiment, was at the
same time busy creating—with it and out of it—his own play."

   This distinctly Pirandellian poet figure is among Abell's most ambitious and most demanding character conceptions, and the role
projects an attitude which appears fundamental to the playwright's
own view of art as well. In performance, the florid and mannered
narrative style peculiar to this character (for example, "a chilly
foreboding congealed into certainty" or "silence settled down in the
darkness of the corners like hounds tired after a hunt") creates a
substantial stumbling block. In the original Sam Besekow production, it left an impression of verbosity and turbidity that even the
great verbal gifts and immense authority of Mogens Wieth could not
erase from the part. Nevertheless, this reflective, "epic" style—in
reality an extreme development of the monologue technique introduced in *The Blue Pekinese*—seems clearly intended by the playwright to serve a dual purpose. On the one hand, the device of the
narrator and his use of direct address provides yet another example
of Abell's continued determination to open out his stage in order to
implicate his audience more directly in the action. More important,
however, the detached and often bitterly ironic tone underlying
Dumas' speeches must be seen in relation to the novelist's
persona—the acutely aware *eiron* (self-deprecator) in whom self-
reflection and self-scrutiny border almost on Kierkegaardian soul-
sickness. "Had Abell been able to concentrate his idea so that the
role of Dumas did not overflow all bounds, a solid success would
have been his," observed *Berlingske Tidende*'s reviewer with considerable insight. "As it is, he trips himself up a bit by allowing
Dumas to say so terribly much." The point is that Abell has in this
play come closer than ever before in his writing to molding a novel
for the stage. Cutting through its dense texture and the opacity of its
language, however, is the agonized cry of the artist to his creation:

Through a forgotten and long-since controlled spontaneity, I fantasized my
way to that sorcerer's apprentice who transformed my airy spell into living
words that create life—your life, Marguerite, and yet, you created it yourself. . . . Save me from my contemplation behind the café table outside
Belle Préférence—your profile in the crowd, the traffic that glides past, I
cannot reach you, hear my voice shouting through the song of the wheels—I
love you, Marguerite. (98)

The theme of love's power over death is thus juxtaposed in *Kameliadamen* with the intensely personal countermotif of the artist's own suffering. Always part of his own creation, he must nonetheless always remain outside of it, continuing helplessly to observe, but ultimately left to his own isolation within "that self-elected freedom that closes in like a prison" (101).

Marguerite, the focal point of the fragmented visions which Armand's reminiscences and Dumas' comments conjure up in the author's study, is also depicted as a much more complex character than the sentimentalized coquette of the original story. This modernized Lady of the Camelias (from whose magnificent gowns every trace of her famous floral trademark was banished in the first production) is the last in the long succession of Abellian "widows" or "ice flowers." Trapped, like the title figure in the early ballet "The Widow in the Mirror," in an egoistic shadow dance of dead ideas and empty social conventions, she is characterized by Dumas as "a lily in ice-cold purity, a love goddess who knew only adoration, and who adored only herself" (18). "The main thing is never to stop," she at first tells Armand bitterly. "As long as the dance continues, there is no time left to think":

No, Monsieur Duval, Armand Duval—with your "I love you" you come springing like a boy through the hedge into a neighbor's garden. But the garden into which you have intruded is a world outside the world. The same words are used as in yours, but here a lie is honest, we know what it entails. No one will get me to step outside this world. Here I have my freedom.
ARMAND. And your solitude.
MARGUERITE. My solitude before the mirror.

(51–52)

Like her predecessor Tordis Eck, however, she is ultimately rescued from her emotional sclerosis—"carried out of the mirror, away from the image that was [her] barren infatuation with solitude"—and brought back to life by Armand, "who with his warmth created a human being, two human beings who became one" (84).

On one plane, Abell's approach to the story of Marguerite Gautier partakes of the same undercurrent of social criticism that colors Dumas' original work. The politically restless and corrupt Parisian society of the late 1840s is seen as a materialistic and hypocritical masculine milieu in which women are exploited and made into "bodies without souls, souls without bodies, knitting odalisques to whom old age represents death before death." The play's principal sound effect, the incessant rumble of carriage wheels, conveys the restless, pleasure-seeking mentality of a butterfly world that takes no notice of the two work-worn peasants who trudge across the stage with their two-wheeled cart in the opening tableau. Like Zeus in *Days on a Cloud*, the masculine divinity who reigns over this mendacious world—the elderly duke who acts as Marguerite's "protector"—never actually appears, but his approach is constantly at hand. With all the clearsightedness and outspoken contempt of Madam Branza, the procuress in *Judith*, Marguerite herself recognizes the doubleness of the moral standard in this opportunistic society, and she exploits it fully in her struggle for survival. She is shown surrounded by "all the symbols of femininity" which this milieu fosters, and which are subsumed in her own personality: the tractable servility of the maid Nanine, the cynical ruthlessness of the witchlike procuress Prudence Duvernoy, and the animalistic sexuality of the bulging Olympe.[20] On another level, however, Abell endeavors to transcend the obvious limitations of these rather commonplace social tensions by nominating his heroine as a mystical hieroglyph of universal human suffering and love. "Marguerite Gautier, behind your closed shutters, it is not yourself you must save but all of us in you" (75), proclaims his Dumas. As the drama reaches its climax, Marguerite becomes "a mortal Aphrodite"—the "victorious human being in league with eternity, the meaning behind eternity that cannot be formed in words" (98)—whose unshakable faith in the power and indestructibility of love transforms her tragedy into triumph. Heard for the last time, the rumble of "the wheels, the wheels around Etoile" conveys to Dumas the image of triumphant chariot wheels—"the goddess victorious!"

Kameliadamen is, as these remarks should suggest, an intricate fretwork of images and themes, by no means all of which achieve equal clarity or forcefulness of expression in the play. This unusual experiment, the last of his works that Abell lived to see performed in the theater, is in one sense a kind of shimmering, suggestive dramatic anagram in which almost all of the motifs and ideas in his previous writing are to be found transposed and interwoven. The play defies conventional classification, but whether one regards it as a "novelistic" drama or a psychological novel for the stage, its compositional logic is associational and is governed by a concern with language and the sound of language rather than with dramatic action in the usual sense. In the theater (at least in the first production) its serpentine dialogue proved difficult for actors to speak and audiences to endure for long stretches (though its run of fifty-seven performances dismisses any idea of popular failure). "One word follows the next in long torrents and cascades. Streams, regiments, and myriads of words pour out and in through Abell's gauze transparencies," ran one review which, in this respect, fairly exemplifies the general critical response. "Sounds were emphasized and words were tasted—evidently for the pleasure of taste and sound alone."[21] Reading the play, however, one is nonetheless brought by its subtle poetic orchestration of voices and by its introspective, almost Joycean exploration of the consciousness of the artist to recall a simple but very valid remark once made about *The Blue Pekinese.* Whatever objections one may be able to marshal against Kjeld Abell's writing, "he nevertheless has words that transform his almost private sorrow into something more."[22]

III   The Scream *(1961)*

"You will discover," Abell reportedly told a friend shortly after having submitted his last work, *Skriget (The Scream),* for production, "that my new play is actually about the same thing as *Melody.* The time has now come to be cheerful."[23] *The Scream,* although finished at the beginning of 1961, did not reach the Royal Theater stage until November 2 of that year, nearly eight months after the playwright's untimely death. Its flashes of wry humor and social satire do, as Abell himself suggests, remind one of his early "cheerful" comedies of the thirties. Nevertheless, this elusive poetic fable, which is virtually devoid of any direct dramatic action, is fundamentally different from everything preceding it in his writing. All pretences to coherent plot development, conflict, and sequential dialogue have now been abandoned, leaving only the rhythm, harmony, and music of what Aristotle calls "embellished language" to bear the play's heavy thematic burden. "The scream which is the dramatic expression of the theme is quite literally left hanging in the air," writes Tage Hind in his commentary on the play. "Vibrating, intense, theatrical—but, at the moment when it is heard, incomprehensible to the spectator."[24]

In performance, this visionary experiment—set in the shimmer-

ing darkness of "a dusty tower-attic beneath the belfry in a country
church" that is inhabited by an Aristophanic assembly of bird-
characters—places severe, perhaps even impossible, demands on
actor and spectator alike. "How good it would be," began one of the
principal opening-night reviews,

> if one could say to all those who have not understood a syllable: stop asking
> for an instruction manual. This is a stage poem, it must not be explained, it
> must be experienced directly, as it unfolds before our eyes, mysterious,
> absorbing, strangely pleasing. But this was not the case. . . . It is so easy to
> accuse this free fabulist of being unclear. But are we not all under indict-
> ment? The theater for what it ought to bring forth, but has not brought
> forth. Ourselves—his audience—for what we should sense, but have
> neither eyes to see nor ears to hear.[25]

Perhaps—though the question invariably calls to mind Samuel
Johnson's mischievous remark about the mystic Jacob Boehme, "if
what Jacob has to say is ineffable, Jacob should not say it." A play,
John Gassner was fond of insisting, "must embody specific action
capable of active materialization on the stage."[26] If—by this basic
standard at least—*The Scream* is not a play in the conventional
sense, it remains what H. C. Branner called "a fairy tale, a fable, a
myth"—a complex poetic fantasy whose richness of possibility carries a direct, subjective appeal to the reader who is prepared to
make the effort to overcome his resistance to its unfamiliar
dramaturgical technique. Underlying and unifying its tangled skein
of associations and impressions is the strong central theme which
links the work to the earlier plays, the reaffirmation of life and
human growth and the repudiation of those agents of conformity,
emotional sterility, and despair that continually threaten to nullify
these positive values.

As so often before in Abell's drama, this simple and familiar
theme finds its expression in *The Scream* in terms of an intricate
pattern of character and image clusters. The play attempts to
explore several interrelated levels of awareness at once, an-
thropomorphic, contemporary, archetypal. The most unusual as
well as the predominant character cluster in it is represented by the
five bird-characters whose comments clarify the unseen events that
are taking place during the Sunday service in progress in the church
below. Two owls, Tuwit and her silent, sleepy mate Tuhuh, have
escaped from their cage in the zoo to the dark church tower, where

they plot revenge on the tame, hypocritical Crow, a traitor to the bird race who is responsible for the owls having fallen into human hands. Tuwit and Tuhuh are joined in their flight by their irrepressible companion Arthur, a loquacious organizer and lady-killer who prefers to fancy himself "an Australian vulture brought home by a seaman"—and whose Norwegianized sailor's dialect often seems as unreasonably constrictive as O'Neill's nautical lingo at its most frustrating. The fifth member of the play's ornithological dimension is Arthur's ornamental conquest Louise—a brainless "pin-up love-bird in green and gold surrounding a milk-white breast" who serves to epitomize the coldly indifferent attitude of the natural world toward the final brutal destruction of the hyperhuman crow by his own kind:

LOUISE.   God, how funny—look at the crow, now the others are tearing off one of his legs—pecking out his eyes—
ARTHUR.   So much of a bird was he in his heart of hearts—he never screamed.[27]

The distinction is an essential one. The scream of the title, a piercing cry heard twice during the morning service taking place in the church, is a strictly human phenomenon—and, as Tuwit observes, "whenever the human circle intersects our winged world, only unhappiness can result" (25). The obvious (though superficial) echoes of Aristophanes' classical comedy *The Birds* have been noticed often enough.[28] Another notable parallel, much closer to home, might be discovered in H. C. Andersen's impressionistic *Fodreise fra Holmens Canal* (*A Walking Trip*), in the delightful episode in which the young poet encounters "two old owls deep in conversation; had they not carried on their discussion in iambics, I would have taken them for real human beings, so naturally did they speak."[29] Disregarding its literary antecedents and multiple borrowings, however, *The Scream* is a singular and fundamentally Abellian creation. Nowhere is this perhaps more apparent than in the Clara Pontoppidan role of Tuwit, the last in a veritable gallery of related figures extending from Kathrine of Lower Bavaria to Anna Sophie Hedvig and on through the Woman in the Yellow Satin Coat. Unlike the majestic but taciturn eagle in a neighboring cage who broods in stern silence over "the modern world picture in which we are all gradually compelled to live on ice-cream and hot-dogs alone" (23),

the sensitive Tuwit has acquired a lively, compassionate understanding of humanity and its foibles during her long years in captiv-
ity:

When I first came to the zoo and was forced to watch existence through a
grating, I understood nothing of what was said around me, I had to listen
my way forward, listen far down behind all the grimaces. Always they say
something they don't mean—but if you listen down underneath what they
don't mean, listen all the way down, then language becomes the same as in
the winged world, there are no lies down there, because there are no words
down there. . . . (87)

More than any other character in the play, Tuwit is revealed "in all
her modest dignity as an image of the intense bond linking all living
things"[30]—a mystical embodiment of that openness and pantheistic
responsiveness to the "song of life" for which this philosophical
drama, quite literally, cries out. Prodded by Arthur, she admits
that, "—yes—I never thought about it before—I—I sense the open,
the limitless, everything becoming one thing, my heaven, my
clouds, my swaying treetops becoming one with all other heavens,
with all that I know—and don't know, but—but have a feeling must
exist" (27). Only twice, however, has Tuwit seen reflected in human
eyes "that same heaven, the same clouds, all that I know and don't
know, but have a feeling must exist"—once in a young artist who
sketched her in the zoo, and now in the mysterious drunkard who
lies dying on the rafters of her dusty church spire.
    Before the concrete dramatic point behind these discursive rumi-
nations begins to glimmer in the shadows, however, a good deal
more philosophical disquisition ensues, as Tuwit and the sagacious
Arthur—perhaps the rough equivalent of Epops, the Aristophanic
hoopoe in *The Birds*—discourse on Man, his refusal to live, to be
part of existence, "to heed the cry that penetrates the wall" behind
his eyes, and his responsibility for finding and fulfilling his own
particular "strophe in the poem" that is universal nature. Their
exchanges represent neither dramatic dialogue nor dialectical argument; they simply take turns at assuming the narrator's role. Only
with the departure of the windy Australian vulture and the arrival
on the scene of the villainous crow—who promptly pushes the sun-
blind Tuhuh out into the daylight to be tormented by the smaller
birds—does an element of conflict begin to color the proceedings.
This glib and egoistic character, whose life as a household pet has

imbued him with all the narrow-mindedness and prejudice of the human race, is also (luckily for the audience) a sharp-eyed, inquisitive, and reasonably articulate source of information about the events taking place outside the tower. The sounds and fleeting visions to which these events are related are comprehensible to the spectator only in terms of the precious scraps of explanation imbedded in the meandering conversation of the birds. He is permitted to perceive more than the crow—the obtuse "realist" who sees and hears nothing—but less than the clairvoyant Tuwit. With her intuitive sense that "something is underway, always on the way up through the beams and rafters" of her tower (38), the anxiously maternal owl provides the play with a unifying focus of sympathy, a dramatic presence in whom its divergent planes of awareness meet.

Viewed solely through the "epic" medium of the interpretative bird chorus and glimpsed only in splintered, dislocated fragments, the actual "story" which unfolds in this drama concerns a typically Abellian moment of human crisis. On this particular Sunday,[31] when the divine service in the village church is to be broadcast over national radio, the regular organist—the schoolteacher's hysterical and neurotic wife—has succumbed to stage fright and relinquished her duties to Dan, the young reserve organist who reminds Tuwit of her sympathetic artist in the zoo. Rather than being an occasion of satisfaction for the young musician, however, the moment is one of bitter anxiety and doubt. Not only has the old organ begun to fill him, as the crow disdainfully reports, with an unaccountable dread of what its ancient stops and keys may conjure up: "suddenly it was as if, he said, something or other inexplicable was underway, and far, far away strange instruments were heard, jingling timbrels and oriental tambourines" (60). Moreover, as though these dire premonitions were not enough, Dan also finds himself deep in a domestic crisis precipitated by his own recognition of a barrier that has arisen between him and his wife Seela. Their marriage has been reduced to a "Sunday ritual" of buttered rolls and terrifying emptiness, and, as Arthur puts it in his cumbersome way, the organist has sought in vain for "the words, the expression capable of reaching across the abyss of doubt that stood between them" (25).

"To play an organ must be like playing on the human soul," Tuwit reminds us, and in his music Dan finally finds the expression that does succeed in reaching across the abyss to Seela. The organist's thunderous performance, an integral part of the play's shock assault

on the senses of the theater audience, is meticulously "scored" by
the playwright in his orgiastic stage directions. Swelling "with almost superhuman strength," the tones of the music

rise like storming armies on their way through a thicket, forward toward
light and freedom, gate after gate is thrown open to unknown horizons,
again, again, as in a dream, an ecstacy, tabors and kettledrums and jingling
timbrels crash against an invisible wall—then suddenly, far away, girlish
voices and playful tambourines are heard. . . . The organ collects its breath
in a roar of sounds, closer and closer come the tambourines, more and more
inciting, blending with cymbals and drums into a tempest of exultant fanfares, and simultaneously the stage is flooded with light and color—but
suddenly, abrupt as an avalanche, the sound is cut off, a deathlike silence
falls over the stage, color and light disappear. . . . then, heard through
darkness and silence—a S-C-R-E-A-M! Slowly the ordinary light returns.
(68–69)

As this rather extraordinary prose orchestration suggests, the
scream which gives the play its title and is the expression of its
theme appears to come, at least on one level, from Dan himself. The
artist cries out in his isolation. The husband cries out in his need and
his love. The lover (for the text abounds in explicitly sexual allusions
to the organ) cries out in his desire.

The cry reaches Seela, who has stayed at home to listen to Dan's
performance on the radio, and she responds by rushing to the
church, with the scream in her eyes, to join him. In contrast,
meanwhile, neither the crow nor his "normal" psalm-croaking
brethren in the congregation below have heard anything unusual.
"The organ ran away under his fingers, that was all, though it certainly was also enough," rationalizes the obtuse bird. One small but
noteworthy exception to the emotional anesthesia of the church-
goers is found, however, in the terrified Jacobine from the Pond, a
village oddity who has obviously heard the scream and is seen by the
birds hurtling backwards out of the church "with eyes as though she
had seen a vision" (71). And so, of course, she has. The usually
overlooked but carefully implied connection between Jacobine and
Seela stands in direct relation to the archetypal paradigm which
holds Abell's rebus together, the biblical story of Jephthah, the
deliverer of Israel who sacrificed the life of his innocent daughter.
Jacobine's history, sketchy though it may be, tells a dark tale of

paternal punishment, of a cruel father who "gave her a ride on a rope from the topbeam" and took from her "the day-laborer she loved." Similarly, though in a less directly physical sense, Seela too is depicted as her father's victim. When Seela's mother left him and later remarried, he bowed to social and legal pressures and gave up his efforts to regain custody of the little girl. As a result, when her mother died shortly afterward Seela found herself abandoned among a family of strangers, and pursued by the unwelcome attentions of her noxious father-in-law Oscar. Although Oscar's philistine family milieu finally lost its hold on her when she met and married Dan, its shallowness and artificiality have—as the morning's clash with her more sensitive husband has demonstrated—left their debilitating mark on her personality.

Seela's feckless father, the man whom the playwright holds responsible for all this spiritual carnage, is of course none other than the nameless drunkard who ends his life on the rafters of the church belfry. This strange figure has, as a matter of fact, *already* died: "This morning when the angels came for me . . . and bore me on their wings," he tells the crow, "A faraway scream called me back" (92). In another of its multiple connotations—as the anguished cry of the victim who is brutally sacrificed for the sake of pride or honor or an empty promise—the scream ("a scream I knew, had known all my life, but never heard") summons him back from death to face and acknowledge his guilt. The resurrection is picturesque, but undeniably difficult to accomplish on stage: *Up out of the lifeless form which remains lying on the rafter, the Drunkard raises his "self," almost transparently pale but with eyes that slowly acquire strength"* (76). Obviously, the fact that he is among those chosen few who possess the ears to hear the scream and the eyes to perceive the visions which it calls up prepares us for his ultimate salvation.

In a grotesque flashback vision that once more revives both the satirical tone and the expressionistic devices of *Melody* and *Eve*, the repentant father, serving the function of a narrator, finally reveals the kind of existence to which he so thoughtlessly abandoned his daughter. This sequence, a comic-strip Sunday picnic enjoyed amidst exhaust fumes and automobile horns at the edge of the road, rivals the grimmest moments in Larsen's melody-bereft marriage and Eve's distressing childhood. Although the role of the infamous Oscar is assigned to the crow, the other members of Seela's family are portrayed as picture-framed and expressionless automatons masked by flesh-colored stockings that obliterate their features. The girl's sole source of sympathy, a kindly and owlish old aunt, is enacted by Tuwit. "They are always going through the motions, just like at a theater rehearsal without props," the resurrected drunkard explains to her. "The one thing you must never take anyone at in this social game, is his word" (102). The point of the scene is by no means new or unusual in Abell's writing. Natural instincts and un-inhibited responses ("the dream of the red jaguar") have long since been suffocated by social clichés. The faceless picnickers keep the implications and temptations of the dangerous forest (where "fauns swing like patches of sunlight in our thoughts") at a safe distance. Viewed through a picture frame, the green jungle seems, Tuwit sadly realizes, "just a wood, green as the green that's served with a lamb roast, and everywhere there are signs with arrows and warn-ings, all about what you must and must not, you mustn't anything, except stay in your frame" (107).

In Abell's last play, however, his familiar thematic antitheses— naturalness vs. artificiality, liberation and growth vs. constriction and stasis, life vs. death—are enriched by his attempt to weld the drama's fragmented but "realistic" contemporary story to an ar-chetypal context, in this case the biblical tale of Jephthah and his daughter (Judges 11:1–11:40). The situation is not, as in *Judith*, that a modern character is transported back in time to assume the role of her biblical namesake, but rather the reverse. Time is a continuum, and Seela, Dan's wife, *is* Sche'ila, the daughter whom the victorious Jephthah offered up to Yahveh after his successful campaign against the Ammonites. Dan's music, his scream, and the strange "jingling timbrels" that he had sensed lay hidden in the key and stops of the old organ call forth the first, fleeting vision of the young girl in yellow robes, glimpsed among muffled forms silhouetted against the roofs and walls of ancient Mizpah. When the scream recurs, under similar musical circumstances, early in the second act, it is again associated with a vision of Seela's biblical double: outlined against the ochre-yellow desert sky, surrounded by a dancing chain of muffled young girls with tambourines, she watches the forest of approaching lances which heralds the triumphant return of her father, the ambitious adventurer who to gain his victory has vowed to sacrifice the first living thing to emerge from his house to meet him. That it is his daughter fails to alter his decision.

Although the literal-minded crow tries to relate her mysterious presence to the fact that she is among the figures pictured in the overplastered old frescoes recently uncovered in their church (the historical "find" that also motivated the national broadcasting of the church's divine service!), Jephthah's daughter is far more complexly involved in the action than this shallow "explanation" suggests. In one of the final and most enigmatic scenes in the play, the Seela whom Dan has just rescued from Oscar's macabre Sunday outing suddenly merges with her biblical self and undergoes a ritual reenactment of her original suffering. Dan is fully aware of their sameness:

DAN.   Seela! Always I have known you were called Seela—cried out your name through the thickest walls—always, always it was you alone I sought.
SEELA.   Your voice called back through time—don't let me go.
DAN. Never, never! I will hold your hand through the storm—
SEELA.   The storm over the desert—when did I first see you?
DAN.   You have seen me throughout all eternity!

(115)

The aim of this rather confusing interchange of identities is, of course, to invest the events of the drama with a claim to universality. In the controlling image of Jephthah's eternally frozen promise—the blind sacrifice of the young by the old who have chained themselves to a dead stone idol—all the thematic strands of this difficult play are drawn together. The "stone colossus" on whose altar the victim is offered up—call it an ideology or a system or God—is man-made, manufactured out of human fear, ambition, "necessity." "He knew it, Jephthah my father, when with the lances behind him he saw me standing in the doorway of the house, knew that the force which confers the power to possess also demands life as a sacrifice," Seela is brought to realize.

Yes, there is a God. At the instant the promise is given, God is created, created by man as the walled fortification that blocks the poem. The God who you believe could command the sun to stand still is the same God you also believe has the power to make us stay in that strophe we dare not leave because of our fear of the new, our fear of the movement under us, above us, forward toward the unknown that we shall never know, but already are a part of. (118)

The crow, spokesman in all his guises for the contractual inviolability of the promise once it has been made, enacts in this scene the role of the ruthless high priest Phineás, who upholds Jephthah's vow and sends his daughter to a death that she will relive again and again "down through hundreds of generations" (121). His life-denying presence is counteracted, however, by Tuwit, who as Anjala—the biblical comforter of Jephthah's daughter as well as the kindly old aunt in the picnic scene—proclaims the mystical nature of Dan's lasting victory. In his art—the only true divine service—and his love, he has found his "last possibility of breaking through the wall" of human isolation and despair.

CROW.   In to that God she calls man-made.
DAN.   No—!
TUWIT.   In to that God we do not call God in the winged world, but call it
God if you like, all the worlds that rise up out of the green depths on the
way through the poem from strophe to strophe, the poem that overturns
your stone colossus. (Bending over Dan.) Play, organist, play—and the
carpenter from Lysekil and the cook from Haugesund will say—that's
art—play, organist, play!

(124)

As the tones of the organ fade and the service ends, Seela, freed at last of the yellow robe that denotes her biblical identity, is seen by the birds seated outside on the churchyard wall, wearing a new dress and waiting happily for her husband to join her. The poetic drunkard, freed of his burden of guilt, can now die in peace: "To you I commend myself, you colorless heaven that in your nothingness embraces all the colors of the spectrum" (127). The Crow pleads for mercy, but his mimicry of mankind has been too perfect; hacked to bits by the myriads of crows convened by Arthur, he is the necessary scapegoat whose execution seems, in the context of the play, to accomplish a ritual expulsion of the human vices that have been transferred to him. The multiple resonances of the symbolic scream—the cry of anguish expressed in Dan's music, the scream of the doomed sacrificial victim, the mystical sense of exultation in life felt by those still sensitive enough to be affected by the sound, perhaps by extension the triumphant cry of the owl as it bursts from its cage into freedom—continue to proliferate. All these implications are brought to a focus, however, in the final cry for understanding and compassion implicit in Tuwit's plea as she prepares to leave her tower to join Tuhuh in the world outside of it:

Arthur, show me the way into daylight, so that I may not be blinded.

These words, the last Kjeld Abell ever wrote for the theater, might perhaps also suggest something essential about the nature of his own engagement as an artist, his quest for enlightenment and his determination, at all costs, to guide his audience in their journey toward the light. *The Scream* jettisons, once and for all in his writing, the supporting principles of the dramatic form—sequential logic, character development, a cumulative sense of inevitability—in order to wrench the spectator out of that illusion of an ordered and static universe which these principles seem to reinforce. In doing so, this experimental work seems virtually to postulate a new idea of "theater"—a mutational collage of voices and music, cries and whispers, disturbing sounds and disquieting silences—that is perhaps irreconcilably at odds with the demands and limitations of a stage performance.[32] Nevertheless, disregarding its structural weaknesses as a drama and its overwritten and often even contradictory philosophical tirades and conundrums, this imperfect poetic allegory comes closer perhaps than any of Abell's previous plays to reaching "behind that shell of reality which is ours" to expose "that reality which created us," the transcendental fourth dimension upon which his writing never ceased to concentrate.

CHAPTER 6

Conclusion

TO Kjeld Abell, the rebel and iconoclast of modern Danish
letters, Chekhov's famous remark that "he who wants nothing,
hopes for nothing, and fears nothing cannot be an artist" seems to
apply with unusual aptness. From the very beginning of his career,
Abell's attitude toward his art was engaged and "revolutionary"—
characterized not by political orthodoxy but by a lyrical, emotional
adherence to the *spirit* of revolt, to the reassessment of outmoded
moral, ethical, and social standards. Although his later plays are
manifestly different in style and approach from his distinctly "social"
comedies of the thirties, one persistent leitmotiv unifies all his work:
the struggle of life against its nullification by false values. For him,
theater was always "a fairy-tale world at war with the world outside." Hence his provocative verbal drama was animated by his
professed determination to confront his audience with the dangerous truths which this "brand-new, alarming world" proclaimed, and
to transform the passive spectator into an active, assisting partner in
the theatrical experience. The variety of approaches and techniques
which he adopted in his efforts to fulfil this purpose has been the
subject of the preceding chapters.

Several distinct phases can be distinguished in Abell's dramatic
writing—provided one keeps in mind the fact that all such artificial
divisions are to a certain degree misleading. His early immersion in
what he called the "wordless theater" of the ballet taught him to
control theatrical space and to exploit the nonverbal means of theatrical expression. As a result, the effective use of integrated visual
imagery remained an essential feature of his work. The initial phase
of his playwriting, represented by his vigorous expressionistic comedies and satirical revue sketches of the 1930s, is characterized by
the young dramatist's mocking confrontation with the conventionality and conformity of bourgeois society. As world war became immi-

nent, however, Abell's verbal arabesques and pirouettes were displaced by a more serious tone. In a second group of "political" dramas, his indictment of middle-class passivity and irresponsibility becomes more concrete and intense; his dramatic focus shifts from the social mass to the individual and the affirmative, existential action that is demanded of him in the face of tyranny. *Anna Sophie Hedvig*, perhaps Abell's best-known work for the stage, exemplifies its author's angry indictment during this period of those who "are neither for nor against but always in between," and who thereby neglect to take a stand against the aggressors who ravage the earth.

In what might be called a third phase of his development, Abell moves from these broader social or political issues to confront the problem of human isolation itself, the ambiguous struggle between life's unspoken, unrealized demands and the forces of alienation and death. In these complex visionary "fantasias"—each of which explores in a different way the existence of an "invisible bond" of communication and compassion between human beings—the playwright experiments with an extraordinary range of expressive visual and structural devices designed to reflect and reinforce his theme. As his career drew to a close, his quest for new modes of dramatic expression deepened. *The Scream*, the last play he lived to complete, carried his calculated rejection of the conventions of dramatic form to its farthest extreme. This elusive poetic collage of voices and music, sounds and silences marks in many ways a distinct departure from all that had gone before in his writing, and as such it seems to postulate an entirely new and more challenging idea of "theater."

As important as Abell's plays are to the development and renewal of modern Danish drama and theater, they represent by no means a strictly parochial phenomenon. Their thematic concerns and innovative techniques alike demand to be viewed against the background of significant trends and styles elsewhere. German expressionism, the modern French theater (especially the highly verbalized, intellectual drama of Giraudoux and Anouilh), and the political dramas of Nordahl Grieg have all been singled out by critics as noteworthy influences on one aspect or another of Abell's dramaturgy. Equally important, however, are the less obvious resonances to be found in his writing. Chekhov's nonlinear and nonsequential "contextual" form; Pirandello's views on the mirror and the mask, on the struggle of his characters for their identity and their existence, and on the bond that exists between them and their creator; Brecht's presentational staging techniques; Sartre's "theater of situation," with its focus on the moment of choice and its rejection of a psychological "theater of characters"—these are but some of the parallels that invite further comparative analysis. In turn, moreover, Abell's later plays may in some respects be said to foreshadow the theater of Beckett, Ionesco, and Pinter, striving as they so often do toward a form of drama which is not necessarily "about" something but is the thing itself, a theatrical projection of an inner human condition ("the materialization," as Ionesco puts it, "of everything we are struggling against").

The thematic pattern of an Abell play (or novel or film or ballet, for that matter) almost inevitably reveals the same underlying system of preloaded polarizations: the open vs. the closed individual; the "fabulist" vs. the petty realist; instinct, naturalness, liberation, and growth vs. social cliché, artificiality, constriction, and stasis; responsible commitment and shared involvement vs. passivity and selfish individualism; the female world of love vs. the male realm of power. Ultimately, this toil of antitheses reduces itself to one fundamental, overriding polarization—participation in the vigor and fecundity of life vs. barren solitude and death. Moreover, we are left with little doubt about where the playwright's own sympathies lie; the melody of life that gets lost in his first play is replayed again and again in all that follows. Partly perhaps as a result of these persistent and predictable thematic dichotomies in his writing, Abell has been criticized by some for the so-called "intellectual poverty" of his dramatic arguments. Recent surveys of his achievement have sometimes tended either to belabor the postulated resolutions he seems to offer to essentially irresolvable conflicts ("through his characters he made himself capable of achieving what he himself was incapable of," runs this type of objection[1]), or else to dismiss the content of his work entirely and thereby confine its significance to its author's skill as a craftsman ("the truly imaginative theatricality which enabled him to play upon the full theater instrument"[2]). Neither view is particularly satisfactory. If by "intellectual poverty" one means the persistence with which Abell returns in his writing to the same pattern of associations, the same concepts and theme, a comparable objection might be lodged—with equal lack of validity—against the other modern dramatists (an O'Neill or an Anouilh, for example) who have repeated their own individual theme over and over again, in a variety of keys and variations. The poet and essayist Stephen Spender has argued that virtually all modernists write about the forces of destruction, the annihilating and annihilated elements in modern cultural life. But they are not content merely to register such a condition, they write about it in order to bring to bear their own private vision of a new culture as society's sole chance for survival. Whatever one's opinion of its applicability may be in general, Spender's theory does provide a rather precise and illuminating insight into the nature of Kjeld Abell's philosophical engagement and purpose as an artist.

Above all, Abell regarded the stage as "the free imagination's fantastic sanctuary." For him, the modern theater was a magical world of infinite possibilities, where time and space, past and present were flexible values, where anything might happen and everything is possible and probable. Its purpose extended, however, far beyond its capacity for limitless theatrical experimentation. Abell's iconoclastic, at times even homiletic mode of theater aimed at implicating the spectator as directly as possible in the struggle of words and ideas being waged within the bounds of this imaginative sanctuary. "Theater is entertainment, diversion, amusement, escape from it all. Theater is literature, tradition, a proof of cultural transference," he once wrote:[3]

The theater is a thousand things. But were the theater not, cutting across all else, a peculiar lightning rod that, instead of preventing the bolt of lightning, wishes to call it down, we could as well pack sets and backdrops into a box and store the whole paraphernalia in the attic, like a puppet show that children had wearied of playing with. But the theater is not for children who become weary. Nor for grownups who think they are grown up. Theater is for those human beings who say: I exist, I am alive.

Notes and References

Chapter One

1. The reader interested in a fuller discussion of the modern theater in Scandinavia is referred to Frederick J. Marker and Lise-Lone Marker, *The Scandinavian Theatre, A Short History* (Oxford, 1975), pp. 204–73.

2. Quoted in *Teatret på Kongens Nytorv 1748–1948*, ed. H. Gabrielsen (Copenhagen, 1948), p. 256.

3. *Teaterstrejf i Paaskevejr*, 2nd ed. (Copenhagen, 1962), p. 30.

4. See Marker, pp. 207–8.

5. *Teaterstrejf i Paaskevejr*, pp. 33, 37.

6. *Modern Theatre: Points of View and Attack*, translated by Thomas R. Buckman (New Orleans: Tulane Drama Review reprint, 1961), p. 10; reprinted in *Modern Theatre: Seven Plays and an Essay*, translated by Thomas R. Buckman (Lincoln: University of Nebraska Press, 1966).

7. *Teaterstrejf*, p. 22.

8. "Realisme—?" *Forum* (October 1935), reprinted in *Synskhedens Gave*, ed. Elias Bredsdorff (Copenhagen, 1962), p. 192.

9. *Teaterstrejf*, p. 71.

10. See the Introduction to *Contemporary Danish Plays*, ed. Elias Bredsdorff (Copenhagen, 1955), p. 7.

11. *Synskhedens Gave*, p. 189.

12. Ibid., p. 193.

Chapter Two

1. Frederik Schyberg, *Kjeld Abell* (Copenhagen, 1947), reprinted in *En bog om Kjeld Abell*, ed. Sven Møller Kristensen (1961), p. 12.

2. On the Balanchine season, see also Svend Kragh-Jacobsen and Torben Krogh, *Den kongelige danske ballet* (Copenhagen, 1952), pp. 387–95.

3. Interview with Esther Scheel in *BT*, December 20, 1934, p. 12.

4. On the Royal Theater production of "The Seven Deadly Sins," see also Harald Engberg, *Brecht på Fyn* (Copenhagen, 1966), 2:61–6.

5. *Berlingske Tidende*, November 21, 1934, reprinted in Schyberg, *Ti Aars Teater* (Copenhagen, 1939), p. 108.

6. *En bog om Kjeld Abell*, p. 13.

7. *BT*, November 22, 1938, p. 8.

8. In June 1958, Abell composed a final ballet scenario, called "Columbine og Anderumpen," for Tivoli's Pantomime Theater.

9. *Politiken*, May 16, 1942, p. 10.

10. See "Bournonville's briller," *Politikens kronik*, November 15, 1935, reprinted in *Synskhedens Gave*, ed. Elias Bredsdorff (Copenhagen, 1962), pp. 194–201.

11. *Synskhedens Gave*, p. 51.

12. Translated by Francis Sinclair and Ronald Adam (London: George Allen and Unwin, 1939).

13. Brecht's analysis of the Riddersalen production is found in his *Schriften zum Theater*, ed. Werner Hecht (Frankfurt-am-Main: Suhrkamp Verlag, 1963–1964), 4:91f. Brecht's play, which succeeded *Melody* in the Riddersalen repertory, opened on November 4, 1936, but it was withdrawn after only twenty-one performances and replaced again by Abell's long-running success.

14. *Synskhedens Gave*, p. 199.

15. *Melodien, der blev væk*, 3rd ed. (Copenhagen; Gyldendal; 1967), p. 7; all page references in the text are to this edition. The songs in the play are by Sven Møller Kristensen; music was composed for the original production by Bernhard Christensen and Herman D. Koppel.

16. Arne Helman Larsen, "Kjeld Abells øjne," published in the unpaged program entitled "Kjeld Abell," edited by Poul Henningsen and printed for the memorial tribute in Radiohusets Koncertsal on September 18, 1961.

17. Mogens Lind in *Berlingske Tidende*, September 7, 1935, p. 8.

18. *En bog om Kjeld Abell*, p. 30.

19. Jørgen Bast in *BT*, September 7, 1935, p. 7. Several of these scenes are radically changed, though not thereby improved, in the Sinclair and Adam translation.

20. *En bog om Kjeld Abell*, p. 14.

21. Ibid., p. 15.

22. *BT*, September 10, 1935, p. 5.

23. Joseph Wood Krutch, *The American Drama since 1918* (New York: George Braziller, 1957), p. 42.

24. *Ti Aars Teater*, p. 148.

25. See Svend Erichen in *Teatret på Kongens Nytorv 1748–1948*, ed. H. Gabrielsen (Copenhagen, 1948), p. 262.

26. *Ti Aars Teater*, p. 149.

27. *Eva aftjener sin barnepligt* (Copenhagen: Nyt nordisk Forlag, 1937), p. 17; all page references in the text are to this edition.

28. The awkward rendering of this speech in the Sinclair and Adam adaptation of *Melody* vitiates the trenchancy of Abell's language: "they shut themselves up in their nice little modern flat with all conveniences as soon

as there's a spot of bother starts, and they leave us to muck along outside, and to peg out" (p. 89).

29. Two of Abell's own stage designs for the play are reproduced in the unpaged program "Kjeld Abell" (1961).

30. *Ti Aars Teater*, p. 151.

31. *Social-Demokraten*, December 9, 1936, p. 6. In a very different sense, Abell was "cleansed" of any Brechtian leanings and reaffirmed as a "living and complete example of the blessing of an ancient national culture" in Haagen Falkenfleth's review in *Nationaltidende*, a paper whose pages had recently been aflame with a fierce campaign against "communist infiltration" (Brecht, Nordahl Grieg, and others) in the Royal Theater. See Engberg, *Brecht på Fyn*, 2:75.

32. *Politiken*, December 9, 1936, p. 14.

33. Frederik Schyberg in *En bog om Kjeld Abell*, p. 16; Svend Erichsen in *Danske Digtere i det 20. Aarhundrede*, eds. F. Nielsen and O. Restrup (Copenhagen, 1966), 2:576.

34. P. 124. The coined word "barnepligt" is an obvious pun on "værnepligt" ("compulsory military service").

35. Svend Erichsen in *Danske Digtere*, 2:572.

36. *En bog om Kjeld Abell*, p. 30.

37. *Teaterstrejf i Paaskevejr*, 2nd ed. (Copenhagen, 1962), p. 62.

38. "Fælleskabets 'melodi' og skriget af ensomhed" in Harald Engberg, *Den unge vredes tid: Teaterkritik 1958–1968* (Copenhagen, 1970), pp. 99–100.

39. *En bog om Kjeld Abell*, p. 111.

40. *BT*, February 4, 1939, p. 8. As a critic Brix, the ardent champion of Kaj Munk, had little sympathy for the *type* of drama espoused by Abell. His disdain for Abell's "easily accessible truths" had already been made abundantly clear in his ironic review of *Eve Serves Her Childhood:* "To be truly charming on a stage, one must be banal. Mr. Abell is charming" (*BT*, December 9, 1936). See also Jens Kistrup, *Hans Brix og Teatret* (Copenhagen, 1969), pp. 154–61.

41. *Politiken*, September 25, 1940, p. 11.

42. *Dyveke*, ed. Sven Møller Kristensen (Copenhagen: Gyldendal, 1967), pp. 16, 44.

Chapter Three

1. *Synskhedens Gave*, ed. Elias Bredsdorff (Copenhagen 1962), pp. 14, 118.

2. *Politiken*, July 1941, quoted by Niels Heltberg in *Anna Sophie Hedvig* (Copenhagen: Nyt nordisk Forlag, 1951), p. xii.

3. Ibid., pp. 53–54. All page references in the text are to this edition of the play.

4. *Politiken*, January 2, 1939, reprinted in Schyberg's *Ti Aars Teater* (Copenhagen, 1939), p. 213.

5. Eric Bentley, *The Playwright as Thinker* (New York: Meridian Books, 1957), p. 200.

6. See Schyberg's review of the Danish production in *Politiken*, November 4, 1939; reprinted in his *Teatret i Krig* (Copenhagen, 1949), pp. 16–18.

7. *BT*, January 2, 1939, p. 8.

8. *BT*, December 29, 1938, p. 7.

9. "Anna Sophie Hedvig taught in Miss Lottrup's School" in Ribe, Abell reminds us humorously in "En Trappesten i Ribe" (*Berlingske Aftenavis kronik*, November 11, 1940), his sentimental reminiscence of a childhood home which, no matter how far one journeys from it, "will follow you in thick and thin, right down into your commas."

10. *Kjeld Abell* (Copenhagen, 1947), reprinted in *En bog om Kjeld Abell*, ed. Sven Møller Kristensen (1961), p. 29.

11. The original phrase," får [verden] til at være li' så purung som altid," echoes the title of Nordahl Grieg's celebrated 1938 novel *Ung må verden ennu være (Young the World as yet Must Be)*.

12. On the manner in which the last sentence seems to allude to the famous slogan of *Politiken's* founder Viggo Hørup—"Hvad skal det nytte?" ("What is the use?")—see Børge Gedsø Madsen, "Leading Motifs in the Dramas of Kjeld Abell," *Scandinavian Studies*, 33 (1961), 131.

13. See K.E. Løgstrup, "Anna Sophie Hedvig" in *En bog om Kjeld Abell*, p. 77.

14. Kjeld Abell, *Teaterstrejf i Paaskevejr*, 2nd ed. (Copenhagen 1962), p. 37.

15. *En bog om Kjeld Abell*, p. 20.

16. *Judith*, 2nd ed. (Copenhagen: Gyldendal, 1969), p. 35. All page references in the text are to this edition of the play.

17. *Berlingske Tidende*, February 11, 1940, p. 4.

18. See Elias Bredsdorff, "Kald det part i sagen" in *En bog om Kjeld Abell*, p. 45.

19. Ibid., p. 47.

20. Svend Erichsen in *Danske Digtere i det 20. Aarhundrede*, eds. F. Nielsen and O. Restrup (Copenhagen, 1966), 2:586.

21. *Teaterstrejf i Paaskevejr*, p. 62.

22. *The Queen on Tour*, translated by J. F. S. Pearce, in *Contemporary Danish Plays*, ed. Elias Bredsdorff (Copenhagen: Gyldendal, 1955), p. 117. All page references in the text are to this version.

23. Arne Helman Larsen, "Kjeld Abells øjne," in the unpaged memorial program "Kjeld Abell," ed. Poul Henningsen (Copenhagen, 1961).

24. "Dronning Bodil, anmeldt af Professor Hans Brix," *Berlingske Aftenavis*, March 6, 1943, p. 6.

25. *Berlingske Tidende*, March 6, 1943, p. 4

26. *Politikens kronik*, March 6, 1943, p. 9.

27. Quoted in *En bog om Kjeld Abell*, p. 43. Both Abell's necrologies of Grieg (February 1944) and Munk (January 1944) appeared in *Frit Danmark*, reprinted in *Det illegale Frit Danmark* (Copenhagen: 1945).

28. Elias Bredsdorff, "Abell," in *The Genius of the Scandinavian Theatre*, ed. Evert Sprinchorn (New York, 1964), p. 468.

29. Reprinted in *Teatret i Krig*, p. 131.

30. *Berlingske Tidende*, March 2, 1946, p. 6.

31. Harald Engberg, *Teatret 1945–52* (Copenhagen, 1952), p. 10.

32. *Teatret i Krig*, p. 134.

33. *Silkeborg*, 2nd ed. (Copenhagen: Gyldendal, 1965), p. 9. All page references in the text are to this edition of the play.

34. Frederik Nielsen, *Dansk digtning i dag* (Copenhagen, 1957), p. 79.

35. See ibid., p. 80, where Nielsen suggests an interesting contrast between the character of Git and comparable figures in the work of H. C. Branner, notably Clemens in *Rytteren (The Riding Master*, 1949).

36. Engberg, p. 10.

37. *Danske Digtere i det 20. Aarhundrede*, 2:583.

38. *Berlingske Aftenavis*, March 2, 1946, p. 6.

39. MacLeish's essay "The Irresponsibles" first appeared in 1940. See Frederick J. Marker, "De ansvarsløse," *Politikens kronik*, April 15, 1961.

40. H. C. Branner, "En Nytaarsklokke," *Politikens kronik*, January 4, 1959.

Chapter Four

1. *Berlingske Aftenavis*, December 12, 1947, p. 6.

2. Interview in *Berlingske Aftenavis*, March 5, 1948, pp. 4–5. Compare the interview with Knud Poulsen in *Politiken* the same day.

3. See Harald Engberg, *Teatret 1945–52* (Copenhagen, 1952), pp. 14–15.

4. Two exceptions to this are the useful essays on the play by Arne Helman Larsen ("Fra *Dage på en sky* til *Skriget*" in *En Bog om Kjeld Abell*, ed. Sven Møller Kristensen [Copenhagen, 1961], pp. 86–92) and by Elias Bredsdorff (in ibid., pp. 53–57, reprinted in English in his introduction to the play in *The Genius of the Scandinavian Theatre*, ed. Evert Sprinchorn [New York, 1964], pp. 466–75).

5. Kjeld Abell, *Teaterstrejf i Paaskevejr*, 2nd ed. (Copenhagen, 1962), p. 62.

6. First published in *Forum*, December 1939, reprinted in *Synskhedens Gave*, ed. Elias Bredsdorff (Copenhagen, 1962), p. 233.

7. *Dage på en Sky*, 2nd. ed. (Copenhagen: Gyldendal, 1962), p. 55; all page references in the text are to this edition. An English translation of the

play by A. I. Roughton and Elias Bredsdorff appears in the Sprinchorn anthology noted above.

8. See "Forgers of Myths" in *Playwrights on Playwriting*, ed. Toby Cole (New York, 1961), pp. 116–24.

9. *Politiken*, December 13, 1947, reprinted in Schyberg, *Teatret i Krig* (Copenhagen, 1949), p. 213.

10. Here and elsewhere throughout the Danish text, Abell's language, though transcribed as prose, often displays the meter and rhythm of a supple free verse which skilfully complements the play's mythological ambience:

> De ønsker fred for hver en pris
> med alt, med alle,
> osse med de skyer
> de burde hade åbenlyst
> fordi de indebærer kimen
> til andre skyers undergang.
>
> ....
>
> Det ville være ansvarsløst
> om man så ha'de nok så megen ret
> at løbe nogen form for risiko.

11. Larsen, p. 89.

12. Bredsdorff, p. 471.

13. *Berlingske Aftenavis* (Brix), December 12, 1947, p. 6.

14. See Frederik Nielsen, *Dansk digtning i dag* (Copenhagen, 1957), p. 90.

15. See Larsen, p. 91.

16. These and other Abell prologues and epilogues are printed in *Synskhedens Gave*, pp. 279–323.

17. *Ejendommen Matr. Nr. 267 Østre Kvarter* (Copenhagen: Thaning and Appel, 1948), p. 23. The play's unusual title refers to the Royal Theater's lot number in the official real estate register.

18. *Teaterstrejf i Paaskevejr*, p. 10 and *passim.*

19. *Politiken*, February 14, 1949, p. 7.

20. Carsten Nielsen in *Berlingske Tidende*, February 14, 1949, p. 4.

21. *Berlingske Aftenavis*, February 14, 1949, p.4.

22. *Miss Plinckby's kabale* (Copenhagen: Thaning and Appel, 1949), pp. 10, 12; other page references in the text are to this edition.

23. Elias Bredsdorff in *En bog om Kjeld Abell*, p. 60.

24. *Fodnoter i Støvet* (Copenhagen, 1951), p. 176.

25. *Vetsera blomstrer ikke for enhver*, 2nd ed. (Copenhagen: Gyldendal, 1966), p. 24; all page references in the text are to this edition.

26. *Berlingske Aftenavis*, November 13, 1950, p. 5. Elling's notice is provocatively placed beside Hans Brix's murderous review of the produc-

tion, which is given the apt headline "Babble." Helge Refn's stage designs for this play and for *Days on a Cloud* are reproduced in Frederick J. Marker and Lise-Lone Marker, *The Scandinavian Theatre, A Short History* (Oxford, 1975), pp. 256–7.

27. *Politiken*, November 13, 1950, p. 9.

28. Arne Helman Larsen in *En bog om Kjeld Abell*, p. 94.

29. Svend Kragh-Jacobsen in *Berlingske Tidende*, November 13, 1950, p. 8.

30. See Nielsen, *Dansk digtning i dag*, p. 92.

31. *De tre fra Minikoi* (Copenhagen: Thaning and Appel, 1957), p. 86; other page references in the text are to this edition.

32. "Kjeld Abell som prosaist" in *En bog om Kjeld Abell*, p. 159.

33. Nils Kjærulf in his Dansklærerforening edition of *Den blå Pekingeser* (Copenhagen: Gyldendal, 1965), p. 138.

34. *Den blå Pekingeser* (Copenhagen: Thaning and Appel, 1954), p. 64; all page references in the text are to this edition.

35. See David Jens Adler, "Himlen over Iselø," in *En bog om Kjeld Abell*, p. 140.

36. *Teaterstrejf i Paaskevejr*, p. 11.

37. Ole Brandstrup in *Berlingske Aftenavis*, December 17, 1954, p. 6.

38. *Politiken*, December 17, 1954, p. 21.

39. Nielsen, *Dansk digtning i dag*. p. 94.

40. See Elias Bredsdorff in *En bog om Kjeld Abell*, p. 63. It is interesting that Mogens Wieth and Bodil Kjer—Abell's André and Tordis—also played Anouilh's Orphée and Eurydice with great success at the Royal Theater in 1946. Regardless of whatever influence the Orpheus motif might have had on him, however, Abell was of course closely attuned to Anouilh's work and provided translations of both *Colombe* (performed 1952) and *Becket, ou l'honneur de Dieu* (published and performed 1961).

41. Tage Hind's essay on the play, "Dialog, monolog, stumhed" analyzes its abandonment of conventional dialogue: see Hind, *Dramaturgiske studier* (Copenhagen, 1962), pp. 77–95 (reprinted verbatim in *En bog om Kjeld Abell*, pp. 118–35).

42. Its size should come as no surprise. The legend that Pekinese were once lions, and that they still retain the hearts of lions and the mantle of invisibility has also inspired others, including Agatha Christie in *The Labors of Hercules* (1939).

43. Carsten Nielsen in *Berlingske Tidende*, December 17, 1954, p. 16.

44. See Arne Helman Larsen in *En bog om Kjeld Abell*, p. 103.

Chapter Five

1. *Open Letters to the Intimate Theater*, translated by Walter Johnson (Seattle: University of Washington Press, 1967), pp. 239, 245, 249.

2. Carsten Nielsen in *Berlingske Tidende*, April 4, 1955, p. 12.

3. *BT*, September 10, 1935.

4. Quoted in *Synskhedens Gave*, ed. Elias Bredsdorff (Copenhagen, 1962), p. 12.

5. For an analysis of Abell's language, see Sven Møller Kristensen, "Kjeld Abell som prosaist" in *En bog om Kjeld Abell*, ed. Sven Møller Kristensen (Copenhagen, 1961), pp. 148–61.

6. These four stories and others are collected in *Synskhedens Gave*.

7. *Politiken*, April 4, 1955, pp. 15–16.

8. *Andersen eller Hans Livs Eventyr* (Copenhagen: Thaning and Appel, 1955), p. 17; other page references in the text are to this edition.

9. Collin's famous letter of December 18, 1833, quoted by Andersen in *Mit Livs Eventyr*, is printed in full in *H. C. Andersens Brevveksling med Edvard og Henriette Collin*, eds. C. Behrend and H. Topsøe-Jensen (Copenhagen, 1933–1937), 1:201–5. Abell treats certain facts with poetic license: Andersen had already been informed of his mother's death (in Jonas Collin's letter of November 30); the version of the letter given in the play omits, among other things, mention of Edvard's labors to publish and distribute *Agnete*. No one would question the dramatist's privilege of rearranging history. However, there seems to be far more dramatic interest inherent in the exchanges between the two men over *Agnete* than the play manages to extract. Collin's antiromantic attack of August 20, 1833 and Andersen's reply of September 24 staunchly defending the right of "the lyric poet to express his own personality" in his work might make an interesting starting point for a less simple, more dialectical approach to this unquestionably dramatic relationship.

10. Henry Hellesen in *Berlingske Aftenavis*, April 4, 1955, p. 6.

11. *New York Times*, September 19, 1956.

12. Svend Kragh-Jacobsen in *Berlingske Tidende*, March 18, 1959, p. 11.

13. *Politiken*, March 18, 1959, p. 21.

14. *Kameliadamen* (Copenhagen: Thaning and Appel, 1959), p. 69; all page references in the text are to this edition.

15. Ole Brandstrup in *Berlingske Aftenavis*, March 18, 1959, p. 6.

16. Tage Hind, *Dramaturgiske studier* (Copenhagen, 1962), p. 102.

17. Ibid., pp. 109, 103.

18. Luigi Pirandello, *Naked Masks*, ed. Eric Bentley (New York: E. P. Dutton, 1952), p. 364. It is perhaps interesting that *Six Characters* opened at the Royal Theater less than four months before the premiere of *Kameliadamen*.

19. Elias Bredsdorff in *En bog om Kjeld Abell*, p. 69.

20. See Arne Helman Larsen in ibid., p. 105.

21. Lise-Lone Christensen Marker in *Roskilde Dagblad*, March 18, 1959.

22. Frederik Nielsen, *Dansk digtning i dag* (Copenhagen, 1957), p. 97.

23. Poul Henningsen in *En bog om Kjeld Abell*, p. 113.

24. *Dramaturgiske studier*, p. 110.

25. Harald Engberg in *Politiken*, November 3, 1961, p. 15.

26. John Gassner, *Directions in Modern Theatre and Drama* (New York: Holt, Rinehart and Winston, 1966), p. 101.

27. *Skriget* (Copenhagen: Gyldendal, 1961), p. 127; all page references in the text are to this edition. Arthur's dialect is almost impossible to re-create in translation; here is the Danish text of the line quoted: "Såh meket fugl vahr han innerst inne—skr-ek, jore han i-kke."

28. See Hind, *Dramaturgiske studier*, pp. 117–18.

29. *Fodreise fra Holmens Canal til Østpynten af Amager i 1828 og 1829* (Copenhagen: Selskabet for Grafisk Kunst, 1940), pp. 125–27.

30. Svend Erichsen in *Danske Digtere i det 20. Aarhundrede*, eds. F. Nielsen and O. Restrup (Copenhagen, 1966), 2:591.

31. The sixth after Trinity, a choice which Hind (pp. 115–16) finds significant in terms of the day's prescribed psalm and its lesson of brotherly love and reconciliation.

32. Perhaps its successful revival by Danmarks Radio in 1971 indicates greater suitability as a radio drama than as a stage play.

Chapter Six

1. See Jens Kistrup, "Kjeld Abell" in *Dansk litteratur historie*, eds. Torben Brostrøm and Jens Kistrup (Copenhagen, 1966), 4:479.

2. Viggo Kjær Petersen in *Modernismen i dansk litteratur*, ed. Jørn Vosmar (Copenhagen, 1967), p. 207.

3. "Teatrets sjæl," *Perspektiv* (February 1955), reprinted in *Synskhedens Gave*, ed. Elias Bredsdorff (Copenhagen, 1962), p. 245.

Selected Bibliography

For a fuller bibliographical account of Abell's own works (especially his published essays, poems, and speeches), readers may consult the extensive bibliography compiled by Arne Helman Larsen in *En bog om Kjeld Abell* ed. Sven Møller Kristensen (Copenhagen: Gyldendal, 1961).

PRIMARY SOURCES

1. Plays

Andersen eller Hans Livs Eventyr. Copenhagen: Thaning and Appel, 1955.

Anna Sophie Hedvig. Copenhagen: Nyt nordisk Forlag, 1938; reprint, edited by Niels Heltberg (Copenhagen: Nyt nordisk Forlag, 1951); translated by Hanna Astrup Larsen, in *Scandinavian Plays of the Twentieth Century,* Second Series (Princeton and New York: American-Scandinavian Foundation, 1944).

Den blå Pekingeser. Copenhagen: Thaning and Appel, 1954.

Dage på en Sky. Copenhagen: Thaning and Appel, 1947; 2nd ed. Copenhagen: Gyldendal, 1962.

Days on a Cloud. Translated by A. I. Roughton and Elias Bredsdorff. In *The Genius of the Scandinavian Theatre,* edited by Evert Sprinchorn. New York: New American Library, 1964.

Dyveke. Edited by Sven Møller Kristensen. Copenhagen: Gyldendal, 1967.

Ejendommen Matr. Nr. 267 Østre Kvarter. Copenhagen: Thaning and Appel, 1948.

Eva aftjener sin barnepligt. Copenhagen: Nyt nordisk Forlag, 1937.

Fire Skuespil af Kjeld Abell. Copenhagen: Thaning and Appel, 1955. Contains *Melodien der blev væk, Eva aftjener sin barnepligt, Judith,* and the revised version of *Dronning går igen.*

Judith. Copenhagen: Nyt nordisk Forlag, 1940; 2nd ed. Copenhagen Gyldendal, 1969.

Kameliadamen. Copenhagen: Thaning and Appel, 1959.

Melodien der blev væk. Copenhagen: Monde, 1935; 3rd ed. Copenhagen: Gyldendal, 1967.

The Melody that Got Lost. Adapted by Frances Sinclair and Ronald Adam. London: Goerge Allen and Unwin, 1939.

Miss Plinckby's kabale. Copenhagen: Thaning and Appel, 1949.

The Queen on Tour. Translated by J. F. S. Pearce. In *Contemporary Danish Plays*, edited by Elias Bredsdorff. Copenhagen: Gyldendal, 1955.

Silkeborg. Copenhagen: Thaning and Appel, 1946; 2nd ed. Copenhagen: Gyldendal, 1965.

Skriget. Copenhagen: Gyldendal, 1961.

Vetsera blomstrer ikke for enhver. Thaning and Appel, 1950; 2nd ed. Copenhagen: Gyldendal, 1966.

2. Books

Fodnoter i Støvet. Copenhagen: Thaning and Appel, 1951. Impressions from Abell's journey to the Far East, 1950–1951.

Paraplyernes oprør. Copenhagen: Wilh. Hansen, 1937. Children's book with illustrations by Abell.

Synskhedens Gave. Edited by Elias Bredsdorff. Copenhagen: Gyldendal, 1962. Major collection of Abell's essays, tales, and poetry.

Teaterstrejf i Paaskevejr. Copenhagen: Thaning and Appel, 1948; 2nd ed. Copenhagen: Gyldendal, 1962. Impressions and theories of the theater.

De tre fra Minikoi. Copenhagen: Thaning and Appel, 1957. Novel based on Abell's journeys to China.

Three from Minikoi. Translated by A. I. Roughton. London: Secker and Warburg, 1960.

SECONDARY SOURCES

ATLUNG, KNUD. *Det kongelige Teater 1889–1939.* Copenhagen: Munksgaard, 1942. Statistical tabulation of Royal Theater productions.

BREDSDORFF, ELIAS, ed. *Contemporary Danish Plays.* Copenhagen: Gyldendal, 1955. Contains introduction and translation of *The Queen on Tour.*

Dansk Biografisk Leksikon, ed. POUL ENGELSTOFT. Vol. 27, Supplement. Copenhagen: J. H. Schultz, 1944. Abell entry on pp. 3–5.

ENGBERG, HARALD. *Brecht på Fyn.* 2 vols. Odense: Andelsbogtrykkeriet, 1966.

———. *Den unge vredes tid: Teaterkritik 1958–1968.* Copenhagen: Gad, 1970. Collection of Engberg's theater reviews.

———. *Teatret 1945–52.* Copenhagen: Areté, 1952. Short, useful survey of postwar theater developments.

GABRIELSEN, H., ed. *Teatret på Kongens Nytorv 1748–1948.* Copenhagen: Berlingske Forlag, 1948. Survey work containing relevant chapters by Svend Erichsen ("Tredivernes nye dramatikere") and Ejnar Thomsen ("Besættelse og befrielse").

GUSTAFSON, ALRIK, ed. *Scandinavian Plays of the Twentieth Century,* Second Series. Princeton and New York: American-Scandinavian Foundation, 1944. Contains an introduction by Gustafson and a translation of *Anna Sophie Hedvig.*

HENNINGSEN, POUL, ed. "Kjeld Abell." Undated and unpaged program for memorial tribute in Radiohusets Koncertsal, September 18, 1961. Includes Abell designs and useful article, "Kjeld Abells øjne," by Arne Helman Larsen.

HIND, TAGE. *Dramaturgiske studier.* Copenhagen: Gyldendal, 1962. Chapters on *The Blue Pekinese, Lady of the Camelias,* and *The Scream.*

KISTRUP, JENS. "Kjeld Abell." In *Dansk litteratur historie,* edited by Torben Brostrøm and Jens Kistrup, IV. Copenhagen: Politikens Forlag, 1966. General survey of Abell's career, pp. 463–80.

KJÆRULF, NILS, ed. *Den blå Pekingeser.* Copenhagen: Dansklærerforeningens udg. Gyldendal, 1965. Critical commentary pp. 109–46.

KRAGH-JACOBSEN, SVEND. *Teaterårbogen,* 10 vols. (1955–1965). Copenhagen: Gjellerup, 1956–67; vol. 17 (1971–1972), Gjellerup, 1973. Statistical yearbook with pictures and commentary; resumed, with plans for filling in six-year pause (vols. 11-16), in future.

KRAGH-JACOBSEN, SVEND and TORBEN KROGH. *Den kongelige danske Ballet.* Copenhagen: Selskabet for Udgivelse af Kulturskrifter, [1952]. Comments on Abell's ballets, reproduces *Thorvaldsen* design.

KRISTENSEN, Sven MØLLER. *Dansk litteratur 1918–1955,* 6th ed. Copenhagen: Munksgaard, 1965.

———, ed., *En bog om Kjeld Abell.* Copenhagen: Gyldendal, 1961. Important collection of twelve articles on Abell; also contains nine-page bibliography of Abell's work by Arne Helman Larsen.

MADSEN, BØRGE GEDSØ. "Leading Motifs in the Dramas of Kjeld Abell," *Scandinavian Studies,* 33 (1961), 127–36.

MARKER, FREDERICK J. and LISE-LONE MARKER, *The Scandinavian Theatre. A Short History.* Oxford: Basil Blackwell, 1975. Two illustrated chapters on "The Modern Theatre" and "Since 1945." Three stage designs for Abell's plays are also reproduced.

MITCHELL, P. M. *A History of Danish Literature.* Copenhagen: Gyldendal, 1957. General survey, with a brief comment on Abell.

NIELSEN, FREDERIK. *Dansk digtning i dag,* 3rd. ed. Copenhagen: Fremad, 1963. Chapter devoted to Abell.

NIELSEN, FREDERIK, and OLE RESTRUP, eds. *Danske Digtere i det 20. Aarhundrede.* Vol 2. Copenhagen: Gad, 1966. Contains extensive discussion of Kjeld Abell by Svend Erichsen, pp. 571–92.

"Rebel of Danish Drama," *Times Literary Supplement,* January 18, 1963, p. 40.

SCHYBERG, FREDERIK. *Kjeld Abell.* Copenhagen: Thaning and Appel, 1947. Short study, in forty-six pages, of Abell's earlier plays; reprinted in Sven Møller Kristensen, *En bog om Kjeld Abell,* pp. 10–34.

———. *Teatret i Krig.* Copenhagen: Gyldendal, 1949. Collection of Schyberg's theater reviews from the period 1939–1948.

———. *Ti Aars Teater,* Copenhagen: Gyldendal, 1939. Collection of Schyberg's reviews from the preceding decade.

SPRINCHORN, EVERT, ed. *The Genius of the Scandinavian Theatre.* New
    York: New American Library, 1964. Contains general introduction,
    "Abell" by Elias Bredsdorff, and a translation of *Days on a Cloud.*
VOSMAR, JØRN, ed., *Modernismen i dansk litteratur.* Copenhagen: Fremad,
    1967. Includes a few pages on Abell by Viggo Kjær Petersen.

Index